FREEDOM
AND ITS BETRAYAL

FREEDOM
AND ITS BETRAYAL

Six Enemies of Human Liberty

ISAIAH BERLIN

Edited by Henry Hardy

Princeton University Press
Princeton and Oxford

Published in the United States by Princeton University Press, 41 William Street, Princeton, New Jersey 08540

Library of Congress Control Number 2001096475

ISBN 0–691–09099–8

www.pup.princeton.edu

Printed in Great Britain

1 3 5 7 9 10 8 6 4 2

To the memory of Anna Kallin
1896–1984

CONTENTS

EDITOR'S PREFACE

FIFTY YEARS AGO, when the six hour-long lectures published in this volume were delivered, they created a broadcasting sensation. Never before had a speaker on this scale been allowed to dispense with a prepared script, and the forty-three-year-old Isaiah Berlin was the right person to inaugurate this risky practice. His headlong delivery, his idiosyncratic voice (even though this made it hard for some to understand him), his extraordinary articulacy, his evident absorption in his topic, the unfamiliar but immediately exciting subject-matter – all this combined to create an impact that those who listened at the time still remember today. People tuned in expectantly each week and found themselves mesmerised. John Burrow, then a schoolboy, records that the lectures 'excited me so much that I sat, for every talk, on the floor beside the wireless, taking notes'.[1] When the series was over, it was the subject of a *Times* first leader, which provoked a correspondence on the letters page to which Berlin contributed.[2]

The lectures consolidated Berlin's growing reputation as a man who could speak about intellectual matters in an accessible and absorbing way, and in his view they also laid the foundation

---

[1] John Burrow, 'A Common Culture? Nationalist Ideas in Nineteenth-Century European Thought', unpublished inaugural lecture as Professor of European Thought, Oxford, 7 April 1996, p. 3. See also Lelia Brodersen's description (p. xiv below) of the earlier version of the lectures delivered in the USA.

[2] 'The Fate of Liberty', *The Times*, 6 December 1952, p. 7; letters, 9, 10, 12, 16 (Berlin), 18 December.

for his appointment five years later to the Chichele Professor-ship of Social and Political Theory at Oxford.[1] There was a less flattering side to this celebrity too, one which was always a worry to Berlin: he was afraid he was regarded partly as a showman, a variety turn,[2] and indeed Michael Oakeshott introduced him (so the story goes) at the London School of Economics the following year, when he gave the first Auguste Comte Memorial Trust Lecture[3] there, as 'the Paganini of the lecture platform'. There was some foundation to this fear, for he became a byword for rapid highbrow speech – 'the only man who pronounces "epistemological" as one syllable'. But this aspect of his public image did no permanent damage to the kind of recognition that counted, recognition of his wide-ranging intellectual resources and his ability to deploy them with unique style, clarity and persuasiveness.

A somewhat crackly recording of just one of the lectures – that on Rousseau – survives, and may be listened to at the British Library in London.[4] This is the closest we can come to recreating today the effect the lectures had in 1952. But there are transcripts (if sometimes very imperfect) of all six lectures, and now that these have been edited it is possible once again to witness Berlin's exceptional expository fluency, and to feel the impact of this early account of his views on liberty, views made famous in 1958 in his inaugural lecture as Chichele Professor, *Two Concepts of Liberty*. But *Freedom and its Betrayal* is by no

[1] In a piece on his appointment the *Sunday Times* referred to 'his famous broadcasts, rapid, vivid, torrential cascades of rich, spontaneous ideas and images' (31 March 1967, p. 3).

[2] The *Radio Times* stressed this aspect of Berlin's appeal too strongly, in his view, observing among other things that he 'is renowned for his fluent and witty expositions of abstract ideas' and 'has a reputation as a conversationalist which extends far beyond Oxford' (24 October 1952, p. 3). Berlin wrote to his producer Anna Kallin on 26 October saying that this treatment was unaccept-able, and that therefore he could not continue to work for the BBC. Evidently he later recanted, but he had been cut to the quick, writing with rare sternness: 'although I may be a mere jolly & garrulous *vulgarisiteur* [sic] this is not the capacity in which I thought I was being employed'.

[3] Published in 1954 as *Historical Inevitability*.

[4] By prior appointment. The call number of the recording is T10145W.

means simply a crude forerunner of a more refined later development. The conception of freedom that infuses these early lectures is in its essentials already fully formed, and this much less dense treatment, especially since it is presented in terms of specific thinkers rather than as an abstract treatise, and includes a great deal that does not appear in the inaugural lecture, is a significant supplement to the work he published in his lifetime.

In my more flippant moments I have thought of subtitling this book 'Not the Reith Lectures'. Anna Kallin, Berlin's producer for the BBC Third Programme, had already been responsible for a number of talks of his. She knew he was preparing to give the Mary Flexner Lectures at Bryn Mawr College in Pennsylvania (as he did in February and March 1952), and she asked him to deliver a version of these on the radio. She was well aware that he would be hard to persuade – for he customarily resisted offers of the limelight – and she was ready to be disappointed. To her delight, however, he was willing. When she heard recordings (now lost) of the Flexner Lectures she had no hesitation in offering him, in addition, the prestigious role of Reith Lecturer, to which he was ideally suited.

But when Kallin's superiors heard of her coup, they caused her great embarrassment by ruling that Berlin was not a suitable Reith Lecturer. I have found no record of their reasons for this view. It may simply have been that Berlin was not sufficiently established at that time, and that the criteria for choosing Reith Lecturers were more conservative then than they are today. There is no evidence, at any rate, that anti-Semitism was at work. Whatever their reasons, the top brass were immovable, and Kallin had to break the news to Berlin. To her relief, he was not offended.[1]

A word should be said about Berlin's attitude to the publica-

---

[1] I cannot at present find documentary confirmation of this story, though this may exist: but I remember being struck by it when I came across it, it rings true, and it is unlikely that I invented it. Useful supplementary accounts of the genesis of the lectures and of Anna Kallin's role can be found in Michael Ignatieff, *Isaiah Berlin: A Life* (London and New York, 1998), pp. 204–5, and Humphrey Carpenter, *The Envy of the World: Fifty Years of the BBC Third Programme and Radio 3, 1946–1996* (London, 1996), p. 127.

tion of these transcripts. Broadly speaking, it was similar to his view of the publishability of his Mellon Lectures, delivered thirteen years later in Washington, DC, and published in 1999 as *The Roots of Romanticism*. He knew that the transcripts ought to be heavily revised and no doubt expanded if they were to be brought to a state in which he could contemplate their appearance in book form in his lifetime. As he wrote to Kallin on 11 December 1951, 'You will easily perceive how it is one thing to say a lot of things in a general fashion to an audience and a very different one to commit words to cold print.' He certainly intended to publish a book based on the Bryn Mawr Lectures, and to do so within a year or two of their delivery, but, as in other cases, he never managed to complete the necessary work, and the long draft typescript on which both sets of lectures were based was laid aside and forgotten, despite the fact that he had revised it extensively. In 1993 I produced a fair copy of it for him, incorporating all his manuscript alterations and an introduction that he had written subsequently, but I do not believe he ever looked at it. Entitled 'Political Ideas in the Romantic Age' (the title under which the Flexner Lectures were delivered), it runs to over 110,000 words, and will, I trust, be published in due course.

I also gave him an earlier draft of the edited transcript of the BBC talks that appears in this book, but this too he could not bring himself to inspect. I thought it almost certain that he would never turn to it, and once mentioned this belief to him, coupling it with an expression of regret. Perhaps out of kindness he said that I could not be certain that nothing would happen: 'Who knows? In twelve years or so I might suddenly pick it up and feverishly revise it' (or words to that effect). But he was already well into his eighties, and this was not a task for a nonagenarian.

Despite his reservations, he did not think altogether badly of the lectures. He thought some were better than others, but he allowed, all the same, that 'tidied up' they 'might make a booklet'.[1] I thought they would do so even as they stood, and

---

[1] Letter to Henry Hardy of 28 March 1989.

backed up my judgement by consulting experts who knew more than I do about the subject-matter. They too found some lectures stronger than others, and some of the interpretations by now somewhat out of fashion; but there was general agreement on almost all hands that publication was highly desirable. I hope it goes without saying that the result is not to be taken as carrying Berlin's own full *imprimatur*; but I do believe that it fairly represents his views on these enemies of freedom, that it will help his readers to a fuller understanding of these views, and that it is no disservice to his reputation to add these remarkable lectures to his published *oeuvre*, so long as their provisional, extempore, informal nature is made crystal clear, and no greater claims are made for this volume than its origins justify.

The BBC lectures are not simply an abbreviation of the typescript prepared for the Flexner Lectures. Nor are they simply a re-run of the Flexner Lectures themselves, as the weekly summaries in Bryn Mawr's *College News*[1] make clear – though it is hard to itemise the differences in the absence of full transcripts or recordings of the earlier version. Berlin himself sometimes said that the two sets of lectures were more or less the same – for example, in a letter of 22 January 1953 to President Katharine E. McBride of Bryn Mawr College:

> I have thought of Bryn Mawr often when I delivered lectures substantially identical with those given under the auspices of Mary Flexner, over the radio in London, when instead of being faced with 100 faces, I looked at a neat functional table and cork-lined walls – and I fear preferred that on the whole: so terrified am I. These lectures have brought in the most astonishing volume of correspondence from the most extraordinary persons who appear to listen to such things and seem to be filled with inarticulate feelings and thought on the subject of history and politics which have come bursting out in the most surprising fashion, and to all of which I suppose I now have the duty of sending some kind of answer.

However, it is clear from the BBC and Bryn Mawr files that the

[1] 13 February to 19 March 1952.

lectures underwent considerable reorganisation before and after Berlin spoke in America, and it would in any case have been very uncharacteristic of him to deliver the same lectures twice, since he was an obsessive reviser[1] and, besides, almost always created his lectures afresh on the podium, even if he drew on the same body of material on more than one occasion.

Berlin's description of his terror when facing an audience is a cue for the introduction of Lelia Brodersen (later chief psychologist at Bryn Mawr's child guidance clinic), who worked briefly as Berlin's secretary when he was at the College. She was doing graduate work there at the time, was therefore short of money, and was picking up earnings wherever she could find them. In a letter to a friend she gives the most vivid account of Berlin's lecturing style that I have seen:

Monday evening I went to his lecture on Fichte & was appalled. He bowed hastily, established himself behind the lectern, fixed his eyes on a point slightly to his right & over the heads of the audience, & began as if a plug had been pulled out. For precisely an hour, with scarcely a second's pause & with really frightful speed, he poured forth what was evidently a brilliant lecture from the little I could catch of it. He never shifted the direction of his gaze once. Without a pause he swayed back & forth, so far that each time one was sure that he was going to topple over, either forward or backward. His right hand he held palm up in the palm of his left hand, & for the whole hour shook both hands violently up & down as if he were trying to dislodge something from them. It was scarcely to be believed. And all the time this furious stream of words, in beautifully finished sentences but without pauses except for certain weird signals of transition such as ". . . & so it is evident that Kant's idea of freedom was in some ways very dissimilar to the idea of freedom which Fichte held, WELL!" I was exhausted at the end, & yet I am sure that if ever I saw & heard anyone in a true state of inspiration it was then. It is really a tragedy that communication is almost impossible.[2]

[1] 'I am by nature a correcter and re-correcter of everything I do': Berlin to Mrs Samuel H. Paul, Assistant to President McBride, 20 June 1951.

[2] Letter to Sheema Z. Buehne postmarked 2 March 1952. Another letter contains a highly recommended account of the experience of acting as Berlin's

To return to the history of the present text: the four chapters of the long typescript are entitled 'Politics as a Descriptive Science', 'The Idea of Freedom', 'Two Concepts of Freedom: Romantic and Liberal' and 'The March of History'. If further chapters were written as a basis for the last two lectures, they do not survive. Perhaps shortage of time prevented Berlin from drafting these, though in the case of Maistre he could make use of a typescript prepared some years before.[1] At any rate, what began as a treatment of six topics, though each topic was predominantly illustrated at Bryn Mawr (in most cases) by the ideas of two individuals, ended up focused on the six figures named in the present chapter titles. Before the final overall title was chosen the lectures are referred to in the BBC file as 'Six Enemies of Human Liberty', and I have adopted this as a useful subtitle. I have also separated out the first section of the first lecture as a general introduction to the whole series, since this is what it provides.

In many ways the editing of these lectures has been similar to that of Berlin's Mellon Lectures, though in this case there were more different versions of the transcripts, more authorial annotations of these, and more caches of relevant notes to rifle. I shall not repeat here what I said about the editorial process in my preface to *The Roots of Romanticism*. The main difference here has been the absence of recordings of all but one of the lectures.[2] This has meant a greater role, here and there, for conjectural restoration of Berlin's words. The bulk of the book

secretary. I am most grateful to Lelia Brodersen for sending me these letters, which are both posted at *http://berlin.wolf.ox.ac.uk/* under 'Letters on Berlin'.

[1] A revised version of this typescript, giving a fuller and in some respects modified account of Berlin's views on Maistre, appeared as 'Joseph de Maistre and the Origins of Fascism' in *The Crooked Timber of Humanity* (London, 1990; New York, 1991). The BBC lecture based on it has also appeared, in advance of its inclusion in the present volume (and in a slightly adjusted form), as the Introduction to Joseph de Maistre, *Considerations on France*, ed. Richard A. Lebrun (Cambridge, 1994: Cambridge University Press).

[2] If any reader knows of the existence of recordings of any of the other lectures – at Bryn Mawr or on the Third Programme – I should be grateful to be given the opportunity to correct the text in the light of these.

rests on uncorrected transcripts made by members of the BBC staff who, naturally enough, were not familiar with Berlin's voice or subject-matter, and found the work hard going; at times they were defeated, and the transcript descends into near-gibberish. (To give just one example for fun, Saint-Simon appears as 'Sir Seymour'.)[1] Almost always, though, it is clear what Berlin was saying, even if the actual words are occasionally in doubt.

As usual, I have been helped by experts in my search for sources for Berlin's quotations, as I record in the preamble to the Notes on pp. 155–6. But my greatest debt, and the reader's – apart, naturally, from that to the author – is to the late Anna Kallin,[2] whose role in Berlin's intellectual career should not be underestimated. She determinedly pressed him, again and again, to speak on the radio. She cajoled and supported him through the lengthy process of recording, and where necessary re-recording, the lectures – a process which, characteristically, he found stressful (partly because it fed his lifelong self-doubt). She was a brilliant editor: 'you perform miracles of cutting, condensing, crystallising', writes Berlin in the letter to her from which I have already quoted, where he also refers to her 'magical hands'. Their correspondence makes clear how important the personal chemistry was between these two Russian-Jewish exiles. Berlin, then and later, needed an intellectual impresario to enable him to realise his full potential. Anna Kallin filled that role with providential effectiveness, and that is why I have dedicated this book to her memory.

Wolfson College, Oxford   HENRY HARDY
May 2001

---

[1] See also p. 169 below, first note to p. 122.
[2] A photograph of Anna Kallin may be viewed on the website mentioned above in note 2 to p. xiv, under 'Broadcasts'.

INTRODUCTION

THE SIX THINKERS whose ideas I propose to examine were prominent just before and just after the French Revolution. The questions they discussed were among the perennial questions of political philosophy, and, to the extent to which political philosophy is a branch of morals, moral philosophy also. Moral and political philosophy are vast subjects, and I do not here wish to analyse what they are. Suffice it to say that for our purposes we can, with a certain amount of exaggeration and simplification, reduce the questions to one and one only, namely: 'Why should an individual obey other individuals? Why should any one individual obey either other individuals or groups or bodies of individuals?' There are, of course, a great many other questions, such as 'Under what circumstances do people obey?' and 'When do they cease to obey?', and also questions apart from obedience, questions about what is meant by the State, by society, by the individual, by laws, and so forth. But for the purposes of political philosophy, as opposed to descriptive political theory or sociology, the central question seems to me to be precisely this one: 'Why should anyone obey anyone else?'

The six thinkers with whom I am concerned – Helvétius, Rousseau, Fichte, Hegel, Saint-Simon and Maistre – dealt with these questions at times not very distant from each other. Helvétius died in 1771 and Hegel in 1831; the period concerned is therefore not very much more than half a century. The six also have certain qualities in common in virtue of which it is interesting to consider them. To begin with, they were all born in what might be called the dawn of our own period. I do not know how to describe this period – it is often referred to as that of liberal democracy, or of the ascendancy of the middle class. At any rate, they were born at the beginning of a period of which we are perhaps living at the end. But whether or not this period is passing, as some people think, it is clear that these are the earliest thinkers to speak a language which is still directly familiar to us. No doubt there were great political thinkers before them, and perhaps more original ones also. Plato and Aristotle, Cicero and St Augustine, Dante and Machiavelli, Grotius and Hooker, Hobbes and Locke enunciated ideas which in certain respects were more profound, more original, bolder and more influential than those of the thinkers I shall discuss. But these other thinkers are divided from us by history, we cannot read them altogether easily or with familiarity, they need a kind of translation. No doubt we can see how our ideas derive from the ideas of these earlier thinkers, but they are not identical with them, whereas I should like to maintain that the six thinkers in question speak a language which still speaks directly to us. When Helvétius denounces ignorance or cruelty or injustice or obscurantism; when Rousseau delivers his passionate diatribes against the arts and the sciences and the intelligentsia, and speaks (or thinks he speaks) for the simple human soul; when Fichte and Hegel glorify the great organised whole, the national organisation to which they belong, and speak of dedication and mission and national duty and the joys of identifying oneself with other people in the performance of a common task; when Saint-Simon speaks of the great frictionless society of producers of the future, in which workers and capitalists will be united in a single, rational system, and all our economic ills, and with them all our other sufferings as well, will at last and for ever be over; when, finally, Maistre gives his horrifying picture of life as a perpetual struggle between plants and animals and human beings, a blood-soaked field in which men – puny, weak and vicious – are engaged in perpetual extermination of each other unless held back by the most vigorous and violent discipline, and only at times rise beyond themselves to some huge agony of self-immolation or self-sacrifice – when these ideas are enunciated, they speak to us and to our age. This is another thing which is interesting about these thinkers. Although they lived towards the end of the eighteenth century and at the beginning of the nineteenth, the kind of situation to which they seem relevant, which they seem to have perceived, to have described with an uncanny insight, is often characteristic not so much of the nineteenth century as of the twentieth. It is our period and our time which they seem to analyse with astonishing foresight and skill. That, too, makes them worthy of our consideration.

When I say that they have these curious powers of prediction, I should like to say that they are prophets in another sense also. Bertrand Russell once said that the important consideration to keep in mind when reading the theories of the great philosophers (other than mathematicians or logicians, who deal with symbols and not with empirical facts or human characteristics) is that they all had a certain central vision of life, of what it was and what it should be; and all the ingenuity and the subtlety and the immense cleverness and sometimes profundity with which they expound their systems, and with which they argue for them, all the great intellectual apparatus which is to be found in the works of the major philosophers of mankind, is as often as not but the outworks of the inner citadel – weapons against assault, objections to objections, rebuttals of rebuttals, an attempt to forestall and refute actual and possible criticisms of their views and their theories; and we shall never understand what it is they really want to say unless we penetrate beyond this barrage of defensive weapons to the central coherent single vision within, which as often as not is not elaborate and complex, but simple, harmonious and easily perceptible as a single whole.

All our six thinkers had some such vision. What they did was bind it upon their disciples, their readers, and indeed even upon some of their opponents. For one of the ways in which a philosopher or a thinker can be great is by doing precisely that. One might almost say that thinkers may be divided into two kinds. In the first place there are those who answered questions which had previously been put, and which had tormented men before, and answered them with a degree of perception, of insight, of genius, in such a way that these particular questions never needed to be asked again, at least in the fashion in which they had been asked before. Newton, for example, was a thinker of this type. He answered questions which had puzzled many men before; he answered them with simplicity, with lucidity, and provided an answer of immense power and coherence. This could also be said of Berkeley and of Hume, and of thinkers who are not strictly professional philosophers, for example of Tocqueville, or of a novelist like Tolstoy. These are all people who answered the ancient, tormenting questions which had puzzled mankind for many centuries, and answered them in such a way that for some people at any rate this seemed to be the final solution.

But there are thinkers who are great in another way, namely, not by answering questions which had been put before, but by altering the nature of the questions themselves, by transforming the angle of vision from which the questions seemed to be questions; not so much by solving the problems as by so powerfully affecting the people to whom they talked as to cause them to see things 'in a very different light', in which what had been a puzzle and a question before no longer arose, or at any rate did not arise with quite such urgency. And if the questions are modified, the solutions no longer seem to be required. People who do this tamper with the very categories, with the very framework, through which we see things. This kind of tampering can of course be very dangerous, and can cast both light and darkness upon humanity. I have in mind thinkers like Plato and Pascal, Kant and Dostoevsky, who in some special sense are regarded as 'more profound', 'deeper' thinkers than other men of genius, because they penetrate to a level where they affect people in a way which transforms their entire vision of life, so that they come out, as it were, almost converted, as if they had undergone a religious conversion.

I do not wish to claim for the six thinkers that they were all, or all equally, men of genius, of dangerous genius, in this remarkable sense. What distinguishes them is that those who followed their views, those who were affected by them, were not affected by this argument or that argument, did not see such thinkers simply as the end of a long period of elaboration consisting of other thinkers of whom they were merely the leaders, or to whom they were merely superior in some way. Rather they were affected by them as one is affected by someone who suddenly transforms one's view of things by placing them in a different relationship from that in which they were before. In this respect, too, all six are thoroughly deserving of our close consideration.

There is another quality, and a more curious one, which is common to them. Although they all discussed the problem of human liberty, and all, except perhaps Maistre, claimed that they were in favour of it – indeed some of them passionately pleaded for it and regarded themselves as the truest champions of what they called true liberty, as opposed to various specious or imperfect brands of it – yet it is a peculiar fact that in the end their doctrines are inimical to what is normally meant, at any rate, by individual liberty, or political liberty. This is the liberty which was preached by the great English and French liberal thinkers, for example; liberty in the sense in which it was conceived by Locke and by Tom Paine, by Wilhelm von Humboldt and by the liberal thinkers of the French Revolution, Condorcet and his friends, and, after the Revolution, Constant and Madame de Staël; liberty in the sense in which the substance of it was what John Stuart Mill said that it was, namely the right freely to shape one's life as one wishes, the production of circumstances in which men can develop their natures as variously and richly, and, if need be, as eccentrically, as possible. The only barrier to this is formed by the need to protect other men in respect of the same rights, or else to protect the common security of them all, so that I am in this sense free if no institution or person interferes with me except for its or his own self-protection.

In this sense all the six thinkers were hostile to liberty, their doctrines were in certain obvious respects a direct contradiction of it, and their influence upon mankind not only in the nineteenth century, but particularly in the twentieth, was powerful in this anti-libertarian direction. There is hardly any need to add that in the twentieth century this became the most acute of all problems. Since the way in which these men formulated the problem, being among the earliest to do so, is particularly fresh, particularly vivid and particularly simple, the problem is often best examined in this pristine form, before it gets covered over with too many nuances, with too much discussion, with too many local and temporal variations.

Let us now return to the central question which all political philosophers sooner or later must ask: 'Why should anyone obey anyone else?' By the time Helvétius began writing, this question had been answered altogether too variously. He was living at a time when, in other provinces of human interest, in the sciences for example, enormous strides had been made, particularly in the late sixteenth century and the seventeenth century, by men like Galileo and Descartes and Kepler, and that group of distinguished Dutchmen whose names I shall not cite, and who contributed so much to the subject, although their unique merits are still relatively unrecognised.

But all these men were overtopped by Newton, whose eminence was unique in the annals of mankind. Among all the men of his age the radiation of his name and achievement really was the greatest. He was praised by the poets, he was praised by the prose writers. He was regarded almost as a semi-divine being. He was so regarded because people thought that at last the whole of physical nature had been adequately and completely explained. This was because Newton had triumphantly managed to express in very few, very simple and very easily communicable formulae laws from which every movement and every position of every particle of matter in the universe could in principle be deduced. Everything which had previously been explained by other means, sometimes theologically, sometimes in terms of obscure metaphysics, at last seemed bathed in the light of the new science. Everything was interconnected, everything was harmonious, everything could be deduced from everything else. The laws in terms of which this could be done were, again, very few and easily acquired by anyone who chose to take the trouble to learn them. One needed for this no special faculty, no theological insight, no metaphysical gifts, merely the power of clear reasoning and of impartial observation, and of verifying observations by means of specially arranged experiment wherever this was possible.

In the sphere of politics, in the sphere of morals, no such co-ordinating principle, no such authority, could apparently be found. If it was asked why I should obey the ruler or rulers of the State, why anyone should ever obey anyone else, the answers were altogether too many and too various. Because, as some said, this was the word of God, vouchsafed in a sacred text of supernatural origin; or perhaps by direct revelation to men whose authority in these matters is recognised through the medium of a Church; or perhaps given by direct revelation to the individual himself. Or because God had himself ordained the great pyramid of the world – that is what someone like Filmer said in the seventeenth century, for example, or the great French bishop Bossuet. The king must be obeyed because this is the order of the world, commanded by God, and perceived by both reason and faith, and the commands of God are absolute, and to ask for the source of their authority is itself impious. Because, said others, the command to obey the ruler is issued by the ruler, or by his agents. The law *is* what the ruler wills, and because he wills it, whatever his motive, it may not be examined at all. That is the theory of absolute monarchy. Because, still other people said, the world has been created (or perhaps, as some said, exists uncreated) in order to fulfil a particular plan or purpose. This view is called natural teleology, according to which the universe is a kind of gradual unrolling of a divine scroll, or perhaps a self-unrolling of a scroll in which God is regarded as immanent. That is to say, the whole of the world is a kind of self-development, the gradual development of an incarnate architect's plan. In terms of this great plan everything in the universe has a unique place, that is, has a place which derives from its function, from the fact that it is needed by the plan to perform this particular task, live this particular life, if it is to fit into the general harmony. That is why everything in the universe is as it is and where and when it is, and acts and behaves as it does. I myself, since I am what I am, where I am and when I am, and in the particular circumstances in which I happen to be placed, must fulfil my function in such a place only by acting and being thus and thus, and not otherwise; by obeying this rather than that authority, because that is part of the plan, part of the scheme of things. If I do not do this, and of course in a minor way I may be able to obstruct the plan, then I shall be disturbing the harmony of the design, and frustrate others, and ultimately frustrate myself, and so be unhappy. In the end the plan is more powerful than I, and if I disobey it too far I shall be crushed by the gradual working out of the plan, which will sweep me away. Some people modified this view and said it may not be absolutely indispensable that you fulfil your part of the plan, not quite inexorable, for the plan is not quite so tight and inevitable as all that, but perhaps it is the most convenient or economical or rational method of securing that necessary minimum which a man needs for the purpose of being happy, or being well, or anyhow in order that life should prove not too intolerable to him. There was still a plan, though you could live to some degree outside it, but not so well, not so comfortably, not so satisfyingly as by adjusting yourself to it.

These are by no means all the types of view which were expressed. Some said that I possess certain inalienable rights, implanted in me from birth by nature or by God (say rights to life or liberty or property), which were said to be inherent in me, clear for all considering men to see. These rights entailed the obligation to obey, and the right to be obeyed by, certain persons in certain ways on certain occasions. Again, there were people who said I must obey this or that king or government because I have undertaken to do it. This is the theory of the contract, the social compact, by which I have agreed to abide in my own interests, because I thought that unless I did so I should not obtain as much as I could in co-operation and collaboration with others. Or perhaps I never actually promised to do this myself, perhaps others promised this on my behalf. Or perhaps this promise never actually historically took place, but is 'implicit' in the way I behave. I behave as if it had taken place, even if it did not; and if I go back on it, then I shall be going back on my word, or somebody else's word on my behalf, and that is contrary to moral law, because promises ought to be kept. Others, again, said that I obey as I obey because I am conditioned to do so, by my education or by my environment, or by social pressure or by the fear of being made to suffer if I do not. There were still others who said that I was ordered to obey by something called the general will, or by an inner voice called conscience, or by something called moral sense, with which the general will is in some way identified, or of which it is a kind of socialised version. There were, again, people who said that I obey because in doing so I fulfil the demand of the world spirit, or the 'historical mission' of my nation or my Church, or of my class or of my race, or of my calling. There were people who said I obey because I have a leader and he has bound a spell on me. Or else I obey because I owe it to my family or to my friends, or to my ancestors or posterity, or to the poor and oppressed whose labours have created me – and I always do what is expected of me. Finally, it has been said that I obey because I wish to do so, because I like it, and I shall stop obeying when and as I please; or simply that I obey for reasons which I feel but cannot explain.

Some of these answers answer the question 'Why do I obey?' and some of them answer the question 'Why should I obey?', which of course is not the same question. Kant's very sharply drawn distinction between the two was destined to form a new period in the history of the entire subject. But what is important is that the entire topic had become a scandal in the eighteenth century. If scientific method could institute some degree of order in chemistry, in physics, in astrophysics, in astronomy and so forth, why did we have to be plunged into this dreadful chaos of conflicting opinions, with not a thread to guide us? Why should some assert one thing and others counter-assert another, some be faithful sons of the Church and some be atheists, some believe in metaphysics and others believe in a private conscience, some believe that the truth is to be found in a laboratory and others that it resides in some inspired teacher or prophet, so that nobody is able to institute the kind of order which Newton established in the great realm of nature? Naturally enough, men's wishes began to move towards the delineation of some simple single principle which would guarantee just such order and yield truths of just such an objective, general, lucid, irrefutable kind as had so successfully been obtained concerning the external world.

One of the people who made the most determined effort to do this is my first thinker, Helvétius.

HELVÉTIUS

Claude-Adrien Helvétius was born in 1715. He was a Frenchman of German origin – the family name had originally been Schweitzer, of which Helvétius is merely the Latin version. His father was physician to the Queen of France and he was himself a wealthy and gifted youth, who through his father and other connections obtained the patronage and friendship of some of the most talented and interesting men of his age – Voltaire, for instance, Montesquieu and Fontenelle. By profession he was a tax farmer; that is to say, he took a very prominent part in the financial administration of France and derived great profits from it. He was a man of charming and amiable disposition, and had many devoted friends. He became one of the leaders in his day of what came to be called the Enlightenment. His principal work is called *De l'esprit* ('On Mind'). He published it in 1758, but it was found to be so atheistical, so heretical, that it was condemned both by Church and by State, and was burnt by the public hangman. He had to make no fewer than three separate retractions of it. Nevertheless it is quite clear that, in spite of yielding to authority, in answer to the prayers of his wife and his mother-in-law, who were deeply upset by what had happened, he did not change his views. When his second book, which was called *De l'homme* ('On Man'), was published posthumously in 1777, it was found to contain precisely, or very nearly, the same impious doctrines.

Helvétius was very famous in his day. He travelled beyond France; he was well received by George II in England and by Frederick the Great in Germany, for he was much looked up to as one of the great leaders in the new enlightened movement of his time. His lifelong aim was the search for a single principle which was to define the basis of morality and really answer the questions about how society should be founded and how man should live and where he should go and what he should do, with the same degree of scientific authority that Newton had displayed in the realm of physics. And Helvétius thought he had found it, and therefore supposed himself to be the founder of a great new science, whereby he could put in order, at long last, this vast moral and political chaos. He thought himself, in short, to be the Newton of politics.

That the problem should have posed itself in that way is natural enough. Let me quote something from Condorcet, a radical Encyclopaedist of very left-wing views born somewhat later than Helvétius, who died in one of Robespierre's prisons in Paris during the last year of the French Revolution:

> As one meditates about the nature of the moral sciences [and by that he of course means politics as well] one really cannot avoid the conclusion that since, like the physical sciences, they rest upon observation of the facts, they ought to follow the same methods, acquire a language no less exact and precise, and so attain to the same degree of certainty. If some being alien to our species were to set himself to study us he would find no difference between these two studies, and would examine human society as we do that of bees or beavers.

And then again he says:

> As mathematics and physics perfect the arts of supplying our simple needs, is it not part of the same order of nature that progress in the moral and political sciences should exercise the same effect on the motives which rule our actions and our feelings?

How was this to be done? Holbach, one of the other authors of the great Encyclopaedia of knowledge, put it thus: 'Morality is the science of the relations which exist between the minds, wills and actions of men, in the same manner as geometry is the science of the relations that are found between bodies.' What is the geometry of ethics? What is the geometry of politics? How are we to reduce these sciences to the same degree of certainty and clarity as physics and geometry? Helvétius thought he had found the answer. Let me quote what he says. In the course of a dialogue between God and man (which, as Helvétius notoriously did not believe in God, is only a parable), he makes God say to man:

> I endow thee with sensibility. It is by this alone that thou, blind tool of my wishes, incapable of plumbing my aims, thou must, without knowing it, fulfil my purposes. Over thee I set pleasure and pain; the one and the other will watch over thy thoughts and acts, excite thy aversions, friendships, tender sentiments, joys, set on fire thy desires, fears, hopes, reveal to thee truths, plunge thee in error, and after causing thee to generate a million various absurd systems of morals and legislation, will one day disclose to thee the simple principles on the development of which depend the order and happiness of the moral world.

What is this but the first clear formulation of the principle of utilitarianism?

According to this principle, the only thing which men wish is pleasure, and the only things which men wish to avoid are pains. The pursuit of pleasure and the avoidance of pain are the only motives which in fact act upon men, as gravitation and other physical principles are said to act on inanimate bodies. At last we have discovered the central principle. If you want to know what it is that causes human beings to be as they are, that causes their characters to be what they are, that causes their acts to be as they are, that is responsible for their loves and their hates, their passions and their ideas, their hopes and their fears, it is this conscious or unconscious pursuit of pleasure and avoidance of pain.

This discovery excited Helvétius a great deal, because he thought it really gave him the key to the whole of social life. Not only did it give him the key to why men behave as they do, but it also seemed to him to give the key to the question: 'What are the proper ends for man?' For if men are capable of desiring only pleasure and avoidance of pain it is absurd to suggest that they should desire something other than what they can desire. If it is ridiculous to ask a tree to become a table, or to ask a rock to become a river, it is equally ridiculous to invite men to pursue something which they are psychologically incapable of pursuing. If it is a fact that they are conditioned by these two forces – love of pleasure and hatred of pain – then they will be happy if they go on pursuing pleasure, frictionlessly, efficiently and eternally.

The question, then, is this: 'Why are men not happy? Why is there so much misery, injustice, incompetence, inefficiency, brutality, tyranny and so forth on the earth?' The answer is that it is because men have not known how to obtain pleasure, how to avoid pain. They have not known this because they have been ignorant and because they have been frightened. They have been ignorant and frightened because men are not by nature good and wise, but their rulers have in the past seen to it that the great flock of men whom they have governed has been kept in artificial ignorance of the proper functioning of nature. This is a deliberate piece of chicanery on the part of the rulers, on the part of kings and soldiers and priests and other authorities whom enlightened persons in the eighteenth century so strongly condemned. The rulers are interested in keeping their subjects in darkness because otherwise the injustice, the arbitrariness, the immorality, the irrationality of their own rule will be altogether too easily exposed. So from the early beginnings of man an age-old conspiracy by the few against the many has been organised and kept going, because unless they do this the few cannot keep the many in subjection.

Man is entitled to happiness, to virtue, to truth. These three things go together, and men have only been prevented from having them by the wickedness of other men, by the weakness of their own nature, by their ignorance, by curable intellectual diseases of this kind. The first duty of the philosopher, therefore, is to apply a kind of social hygiene, to cure people of these easily remediable vices.

Ethics is a kind of technology, for the ends are all given. If you ask 'Why should we do what we do?' the answer is: 'Because we are made to do it by nature, because we cannot function otherwise.' If the ends are given there is no need to investigate those further. The only business of the expert, or the philosopher, is simply to create a universe in which the ends which men have to seek because they cannot help it are obtained with the least pain, most efficiently, most rapidly, most economically. Helvétius says as much. He says that the philosopher is really the architect of the edifice (he means the builder). The plan is there already, because it is discovered in nature; the plan is the seeking of pleasures and the avoidance of pain.

The 'physiocratic' philosophers, who were the leading economists of the eighteenth century, similarly say: Legislation is not the making of laws (that would be more properly called 'legisfaction'), legislation is the translation into legal terms of something which is to be found in nature: ends, purposes. The true ends of man are given; they can be discovered, as the laws of physics have been discovered; and the answer to the question why I should obey this or that king, this or that government, will simply be demonstrable in the way in which the laws of physics are demonstrable. If this or that course of action leads to greater happiness – if, that is, it conforms to the ends set for us by nature – then it is good, and if it detracts from happiness or frustrates it in some way, then it is bad. This is the simple rule of truth, and it ought to be applied everywhere.

Unlike some other thinkers of the eighteenth century, Helvétius did not have too high an opinion of human nature, in the sense of thinking man naturally benevolent. He thinks him neither benevolent nor malevolent, but infinitely flexible and pliable; a kind of natural stuff which nature and circumstances, but above all education, shape as they will. He therefore thinks that it is of no use merely to try to improve mankind by argument. The purpose of reform is to establish new institutions designed to maximise pleasure and minimise pain – to make people as happy as possible and eliminate all the causes of misery such as ignorance or injustice. But it is impossible to do this by precept. It is impossible to do it even by example. Preaching alone will not achieve much, because men are too ignorant, too blind; they are slaves to their passions, they are slaves to their own habits, they are slaves to meaningless and irrational loyalties. All the preaching of all the Christian preachers in the past has done little good because men are what they are, because of their evil education, their sad circumstances, their poverty, weakness, ignorance, fears – all the factors which have twisted them from their true purpose, which have made of them natural cripples.

How is this to be remedied? Only by artificial manipulation. Helvétius does not believe in automatic progress. Some celebrated thinkers of the eighteenth century did believe in that. The great minister Turgot and his friend Condorcet certainly believed in eternal progress: Helvétius did not. He supposes that there will be progress if a sufficient number of enlightened men with resolute wills and with a disinterested passion to improve mankind set themselves to promote it, above all if they convert the rulers of mankind – the kings, the ministers – and teach them the art of government, for government is certainly an art. It is the art of pursuing happiness. Like other arts it requires knowledge. Just as a man who wishes to build a bridge has to acquire a good deal of mathematics, mechanics, physics and so forth, so a man about to rule a State must know a considerable amount about anthropology, sociology, psychology, and indeed morals. Only when he discovers how men in fact function, what the laws which regulate conduct are, is he in a position to produce that which he wishes to produce. Without this he will make dreadful blunders and plunge mankind into miseries which are worse than his earlier state. In the late eighteenth century there was a reasonable hope that some of the rulers of the time would be amenable to this view of philosophical advice: Frederick the Great of Prussia, perhaps Catherine the Great in Russia, certainly Joseph II in Austria were obviously susceptible to this kind of enlightened teaching.

How is it to be achieved? What is the philosopher to do? How is he to transform the world? Not by preaching, because men will not listen. He must compass his purposes by much more drastic means. He must do so by legislation and by inventing a system of sticks and carrots for the human donkey. The philosopher, when he is in power, must create an artificial system of rewards and punishments which will reward men whenever they do what in fact leads to greater happiness, and punish them when in fact they do that which diminishes it. What human motives are is totally irrelevant. It does not in the least matter whether people contribute to happiness because they are benevolent and approve of it, or from some self-interested, base, mean motive of their own. It does not matter whether people prevent human happiness because they are malignant or vicious, or because they are ignorant blunderers or idealistic fools – the damage they do will be identical in either case, and so will the good. Therefore we must abandon all discussion of motives, which is really neither here nor there. It is of no use to try to operate against human prejudices, against human superstitions, because they can be cured only in some very long run. In the short run these things are too ingrained, and therefore, as the Italian thinker Pareto advised so cynically in the twentieth century, 'Do not fight prejudice; use it.'

That is precisely what Helvétius says. We, the enlightened reformers, must not try to convert people by reasoning, because their reason is not powerful enough, in the conditions of today, owing to the dreadful misgovernment of the past, to understand what it is that we tell them. We must substitute 'the language of interest', as he puts it, 'for the tone of injury'. Do not complain, appeal to interest.

'I do not care', said Helvétius, 'if men be vicious so long as they are intelligent … Laws will do everything.' Intelligent judges of their own interests, that is. That men principally pursue pleasure and avoid pain, and that the chief or only purpose of government is to make men happy – this, whether true or false, right or wrong, is a very ancient human doctrine, for which the eighteenth century can claim little originality. What is relatively new is the combination with this of the notion of using men's natural propensities without worrying about the moral or spiritual quality of these propensities or motives. This too is old: as old as Plato, the Assassins, or Machiavelli, or the practice of many religious sects and communities; but the alliance of it with rationalism, materialism, hedonism, belief in science, reason and a particular view of individualism is new. It is this that forms the heart of modern utilitarianism.

The legislator must use vices and weaknesses and play on

vanities as well as the better feelings and worthier attributes of
men. To get effective action he must make it worth men's while
to do the things he wants them to do, not explain why he does
it; make them do it whether they want to or not; and then,
when, as a result of the social conditioning effected by the laws
established by the enlightened philosophers, enough men have
for a sufficient length of time done nothing but what contributes
to happiness, then, in fact, they will insensibly acquire new and
beneficent habits. It is their bad present habits which cause the
misery, and it is their new good habits which will make them
happy. They will not know how they will be making themselves
happy; they may not, for a while at least, understand the
working of their own new ways of living; but in fact they will be
acquiring habits which will automatically produce happiness.
The automatic production of happiness through the conditioning of society by men who have grasped the few, necessary rules
about the right government of mankind, rules which can only be
obtained by scientific observation, perhaps scientific experiment,
and the application of reason to nature – that is the way to
educate mankind. After the proper coercive legislation has been
established it is the turn of the educator. Now he need no longer
be afraid of being stoned by his ignorant and outraged pupils.
Once the laws protect him, he will be able safely to teach them
virtue, knowledge and happiness. He will be able to teach them
how to live. He will be able to explain to them why it is
reasonable for them, for example, to pursue pleasure and avoid
pain. He can explain to them why it is wrong to be an ascetic or
a monk, why it is irrational, the product of misunderstanding of
nature, to try to mortify the flesh or to be gloomy or to be
melancholy. So gloom and melancholy will be driven from the
earth: everybody will become joyous, harmonious and happy.

Helvétius gives precise instructions to his future educators.
They must not waste time on history because history is nothing
but the tale of the crimes and the follies of mankind. It may have
certain lessons to teach us – one may teach history if it is only to
show why it is that humanity, as a result of being ruled by
knaves, as a result of being duped too much by its earlier rulers,
has not done as well as it might. But to learn or to teach history

for its own sake is surely absurd. Indeed, it is absurd to teach or do *anything* for its own sake. For the only end or purpose of action is to render people happy – which is, in brief, the doctrine of utilitarianism.

Similarly, the teaching of classical languages must be abandoned, for they are dead and of no practical interest to us now. All interest is practical interest. What people must be taught, consequently, are the sciences and the arts, and among the arts is that of being a citizen. There is to be no 'pure' learning; for nothing 'pure', without useful application, is desirable. 'Pure' learning is simply an old, medieval survival, something which derives from the days when ignorant men taught other ignorant men that there were certain things which were worth doing for their own sakes, for which no utilitarian reason could be given. Nowadays there is no need to do anything for which no reason can be given, and there must be a reason for doing whatever is to be done. The reason is the pursuit of happiness.

One of the direct consequences of this doctrine is an odd corollary about human rights. For generations men preached that every man has certain inalienable rights. It was one of the basic beliefs in the Christian tradition that man has an immortal soul, and because he has an immortal soul he must not be trampled on by other men. Men's souls – their reason – are sparks of a divine being, and in virtue of this they have certain 'natural' rights. They have the right to exercise their reason, and to enjoy certain things and be given certain things, in virtue of being sentient, being rational, and these rights are implanted in them by God or by nature. Eighteenth-century philosophers too talked a great deal about rights and indeed believed in them very strongly, but of course this is not consistent with a really thoroughgoing utilitarianism. To have a right which nobody may impinge upon, to have a right which nobody may trample, to have a right to do or be or have this or that, whether anybody likes it or not, is an obstacle to the transformation of society in the direction of the greatest happiness for the greatest number. If I have what used to be called an imprescriptible right to, let us say, property, and even more to life itself, and to that limited degree of liberty which was usually recognised as being neces-sary for individuals – if I have such rights then the legislator, in trying to plan the world, may find himself faced with the obstacle of not being permitted to take something away from me which he needs to take away in order to produce a smooth, harmonious, completely frictionless society. But for a utilitarian this is clearly irrational. If the sole criterion of action is happiness and unhappiness, these odd rights which stick out in an obstinate way, and may not be smoothed over by the legislator, must be flattened out. Therefore, while of course Helvétius would maintain that everything which a human being naturally needs will be provided for in a benevolent State in which the legislator is the principal moving force, yet for him the persistence of rights which are absolute, which nothing may overcome, which are there whether other people like it or not, are made happy by them or not, are simply so many irrational survivals.

This is exactly what Bentham did eventually say. Bentham was a complete disciple of Helvétius, and although the word 'utilitarianism' is normally associated with him, I think it is fair to say that there is little – among the cardinal ideas, at least – in Bentham which does not stem directly from Helvétius. Bentham acknowledged intellectual debts very freely and generously, and he said that he had learned much from Helvétius. Even this seems to me to be an understatement.

How is the good, new society to be organised? Certainly it cannot be a democracy, for people are often stupid and often vicious, and we know that if we are guided by public opinion we shall seldom get anything done, because men have dwelt in darkness too long to be able to know what to do when they suddenly find themselves in the light of day. Men are liberated slaves, and for a long, long time must be guided by enlightened leaders, enlightened managers of human society. This is very much the view of the eighteenth-century liberals before Rous-seau. 'Woe to us', says Voltaire, 'if the masses start reasoning'; and again, 'The people are cattle and what they need is a yoke, a goad and fodder.' In the *Encyclopédie* – the great liberal encyclopaedia which Diderot and d'Alembert edited, the most progressive document of its time, which got its editors into trouble with the clerical censorship in Paris – under the article entitled 'multitude' you will find the following passage: 'in intellectual questions [the masses'] voice is full of malignity, stupidity, inhumanity, perversity, prejudice ... it is ignorant and idiotic ... Beware of it in moral questions: it is incapable of noble or strong deeds ... heroism in its eyes is madness.' There is much praise for what was conceived, without much accurate knowledge of the facts, as the Chinese system, in which the mandarins, who alone are wise, do not listen to the masses, but gradually guide them towards a happier and freer and more enlightened existence by instituting laws which these masses do not understand, but by which they are insensibly drawn in a good direction, namely towards their own happiness.

The one principle to which Helvétius clings tenaciously is that education and laws can do anything. There was a great deal of discussion in the eighteenth century about what the factors are that most effectively condition men. Man is regarded by almost all the *philosophes* as an object in nature. They tend to look upon the notion of the immortal soul, which is something quite different from matter, as an obscurantist survival from an earlier period before the sciences had become dominant, when figments were invented to account for phenomena whose true causes had not yet been discovered. The soul is one of those figments and does not tell us what the real factors are which make men what they are. Some said that environment was the most important; others, the chemistry of the human body. Some, like Montesquieu, thought that climate was of cardinal importance, or kinds of soil or social institutions; and some, like Helvétius, declared that those factors had been much exaggerated, and that it was education which could transform anybody into almost anything. This became one of the central doctrines of the *philosophes*, whereby man is infinitely malleable, infinitely flexible. He is a piece of clay in the hands of the potter to mould as he pleases; that is why it is criminal irresponsibility to abandon man to his own devices and to let the ignorant and the malevolent deceive him into obedience, which does not in fact guarantee those ends which he really desires to achieve.

For Helvétius it is 'interest' alone that rules mankind; and this is very relative, for the interest of the ruler is not the same as the interest of the ruled, and the interest of men living in cold climates is not the same as the interest of those who live in warm ones. Nevertheless, it is always interest which is the central conditioning force. He brings this out in an amusing little parable. He asks us to imagine what the minute little gnats or flies who live in the high grass must feel about other animals which occur in their world. They see a large beast, to our eyes a sheep peacefully browsing in a meadow, and they say:

> Let us flee from this greedy and cruel animal, this monster in whose voracious jaws we and our cities will be swallowed up. Why can it not behave like lions and tigers? These kindly animals do not destroy our dwellings; they do not batten upon our blood. Just avengers of crime, they punish sheep for the cruelty sheep inflict upon us.

This is how the universe looks to a fly in the grass. This, no doubt, *mutatis mutandis*, is how the universe looks to every other creature in the universe from its own peculiar point of view. The business of the legislator is so to transform human beings that they shall no longer be preyed upon by ignorance, that their interest shall in fact coincide with what they think to be that interest, that their interest – which is the pursuit of pleasure and the avoidance of pain – shall in fact represent itself to them as such, and they shall not, in short, regard things as useful to them which are in fact useless. They shall not, indeed, suppose that sheep are cruel and bloodthirsty and tigers dignified and kind. They shall see things in their true light. They can see things in their true light only if, like scientists, they understand what the universe consists of, how it is governed, where it is going.

One thing is clear: in the kind of universe which Helvétius depicts there is little or no room for individual liberty. In his world men may become happy, but the notion of liberty eventually disappears. It disappears because liberty to do evil disappears, since everyone has now been conditioned to do only what is good. We have become like animals trained to seek only that which is useful to us. In this condition liberty, if it includes any licence to freewheel, the liberty to do now this, now that, to be able to choose even to destroy ourselves, if we want to – that kind of liberty will be gradually weeded out altogether by successful education.

Let me dwell a little on the presuppositions of this kind of system – this Brave New World (for that is what it comes to). To begin with, all questions of value are factual, and the answers discoverable by observation and reasoning. Ethics and politics are natural sciences. Some people are better at discovering their laws than others. There is such a thing as specific moral and political knowledge and skill, which specialists must have. These specialists should be given supreme power. Secondly, all ulti-mate ends are compatible with each other. They cannot clash. This proposition has often been refuted by human experience. For example, liberty, which is an ultimate purpose of some, has at times been found to be incompatible with equality, which is often an ultimate goal for others. It is difficult to see why honour should always and automatically be compatible with patriotism. The great tragedies – those written by the Greek dramatists as well as those of more modern days – are largely concerned with the fatal collision of values which cannot be reconciled. Precisely this was denied in the eighteenth century, because the most widespread belief of that age looked on nature as harmonious, and to say that nature was a harmony must mean to say that nothing real or valuable in it can conflict with anything else which is real or valuable. In fact this belief rests on a false analogy from logic and geometry. Just as in logic and in geometry no true proposition can be incompatible with any other true proposition, so no value in the moral universe, if the moral universe is a harmony of which there is a science, can conflict with any other value, and Condorcet can say with great firmness that 'nature binds by an unbreakable chain truth, happiness and virtue'. From this it follows that whoever knows the truth completely is also virtuous and happy. Scientists know the truth, therefore scientists are virtuous, therefore scientists can make us happy, therefore let us put scientists in charge of everything. What we need is a universe governed by scientists, because to be a good man, to be a wise man, to be a scientist, to be a virtuous man are, in the end, the same thing. There is a great European tradition which supports this view, whereby scientific government is thought to be the best, and reformers are always, like H. G. Wells, asking angrily why we should not be governed by an élite of scientists. This attitude dates from the eighteenth century, when truth, happiness and virtue were regarded as incapable of conflict, since in the harmony of nature no values can conflict, and so all tragedy must be due to error. There is nothing inherently tragic in the world; all tragedy and conflict are curable and composable.

A further presupposition is that man is one with – continuous with – nature, and therefore there can be such a thing as a science of man; that man, like everything in nature, is malleable, plastic and alterable. This too may be questioned, but certainly the *philosophes* believed it. The Baron d'Holbach tells us that 'education is simply the agriculture of the mind': to govern man is like breeding animals. Hence, since ends are given and man is mouldable, the problem becomes a purely technological one: how to adjust men in such a way that they will live in peace, prosperity and harmony. Certainly men's interests do not automatically coincide. They will have to be adjusted, and this business of adjusting is the business of the legislator. As Helvétius says, the happiness of one man is not necessarily connected with the happiness of others. Social pressure and the philosopher – the enlightened philosopher – will link them. Hence the need for the despotism of an élite of scientists.

'And why not?' it may be asked. The great physiocrat Le Mercier de la Rivière did reason just like that: 'Euclid is a veritable despot, and the truths of geometry which he has bequeathed to us are truly despotic laws. The despotism of these laws and the personal despotism of the legislator are one and the same. They are the irresistible power of evidence.' If geometers may be despotic, why not philosophers? If we do not wish to escape from the truths of geometry, why from the truth of philosophers? Nature, and she alone, teaches philosophers what the true ends of men are. True, nature at all times speaks with too many voices. She said to Spinoza that she was a logical system, but to Leibniz that she was a congeries of souls. She said to Diderot that the world was a machine with cords, pulleys and springs, whereas to Herder she said that it was an organic living whole. To Montesquieu she talked about the infinite value of variety; to Helvétius of unalterable uniformity. To Rousseau she declared that she had been perverted by civilisations, sciences and the arts; whereas to d'Alembert she promised to reveal their secrets. Condorcet and Paine perceived that she implants inalienable rights in man; to Bentham she says this is mere 'bawling upon paper' – 'nonsense upon stilts'. To Berkeley she reveals herself as the language of God to man. To Holbach she said that there was no God and Churches were conspiracies. Pope, Shaftesbury, Rousseau see nature as a marvellous harmony. Hegel sees her as a glorious field in which great armies clash by night. Maistre sees her as an agony of blood and fear and self-immolation.

What is nature? What is meant by 'natural'? It is a good question. Leslie Stephen tells us that an eighteenth-century English traveller in France once remarked that it was unnatural for soldiers to dress in blue, except, indeed, the Artillery or the Blue Horse. It is evident that nature speaks with too many different voices, and if we are taking instruction from nature we shall have too many conflicting lessons, and there will be no final solution, never the beginning of one. Helvétius was quite clear about what nature taught him. He *knew* that nature told him that the only thing which men could do and should do was to pursue pleasure and avoid pain, and upon this he erected the utilitarian system which, armed with the best will in the world, inspired by the purest of motives, directed as it was against injustice, against ignorance, against arbitrary rule, against all the horrors with which the eighteenth century was still filled, leads directly to what is ultimately a kind of technocratic tyranny. For the tyranny of ignorance, of fear, of superstitious priests, of arbitrary kings, of all the bogies fought by eighteenth-century enlightenment it substitutes another tyranny, a technological tyranny, a tyranny of reason, which, however, is just as inimical to liberty, just as inimical to the notion that one of the most valuable things in human life is choice for the sake of choice, not merely choice of what is good, but choice as such. It is inimical to this and in this way has been used as the justification both for Communism and for Fascism, for almost every enactment which has sought to obstruct human liberty and to vivisect human society into a single, continuous, harmonious whole, in which men are intended to be devoid of any degree of individual initiative. It is a very tight, well-built system; there is no room to move in it. Perhaps it can produce happiness; but it is not clear – it was not clear even in the eighteenth century, and certainly has not become clearer subsequently – that happiness is the sole value which men seek.

ROUSSEAU

Starting from unlimited freedom I arrive at unlimited despotism.

Shigalev in Dostoevsky's *The Devils*

THE CELEBRATED HISTORIAN, Lord Acton, once observed about Jean Jacques Rousseau that he 'had produced more effect with his pen than Aristotle, or Cicero, or Saint Augustine, or Saint Thomas Aquinas, or any other man who ever lived'. And this observation, although obviously exaggerated, nevertheless conveys something which is not totally untrue. Against it may be cited the remark of Madame de Staël, who said: 'Rousseau said nothing new, but set everything on fire.'

What constitutes the greatness of Rousseau? Why is he regarded as an important thinker? What did he say? Did he make any new or original discoveries? Did he really say nothing new (is Madame de Staël right?), and if he did not, how is it that such words as Acton's can be applied to him at all?

Some say that his genius lies only in his wonderful eloquence, his hypnotic style, for example in the prose of the *Confessions*, a book very difficult for anyone to put down, a book which has had more effect upon readers than almost any similar work of literature. But was there then really nothing new in what Rousseau said? Was it really only old wine in new bottles? Some place his originality in the fact that, whereas previous thinkers addressed themselves to reason, Rousseau glorifies the passions. But this is scarcely true. There is a great deal about passion and sentiment in Diderot and Helvétius, in Shaftesbury and Hume, who always say that, so far from suppressing men's feelings, as the more austere religions, and also philosophers like Plato and

Spinoza, had demanded, man must not curb or maim his spontaneous nature. Certainly the emotions may have to be canalised or guided, but on no account must they be suppressed. On the contrary, more than any other thinkers who ever lived, the school of so-called empiricist thinkers in the eighteenth century stressed the value of feeling, of human spontaneity and warmth. No writer is more passionate, and indeed at times more sentimental, on that subject than Diderot.

If we look at Rousseau's writings, to all appearance the exact opposite is the case. Rousseau is not at all in favour of unbridled feeling. On the contrary, he says – and he has a great philosophical tradition behind him – that sentiments divide people, whereas reason unites them. Sentiments, feelings are subjective, individual, vary from person to person, country to country, clime to clime: whereas reason alone is one in all men, and alone is always right. So that this celebrated distinction, according to which Rousseau is the prophet of feeling against cold rationalism, is certainly, on the evidence of his writings, fallacious.

There are, according to Rousseau, certain questions about morals and politics, about how to live, what to do, whom to obey, to which many conflicting answers have been given by the accumulation of human feelings, prejudices, superstitions, played on by various causal – natural – factors, which have made men through the centuries say now this, now that. But if we are to obtain true answers to these questions, then this is not the way to do it. We must ask the questions in such terms as make them answerable; and that can only be done by means of reason. Just as in the sciences a true answer given by one scientist will be accepted by all other scientists who are equally reasonable, so in ethics and politics the rational answer is the correct answer: the truth is one, error alone is multiple.

This is all perfectly commonplace. Few philosophers have failed to say something of the kind, and Rousseau simply repeats the opinions of his predecessors in saying that it is reason which is the same in all men, and unites, and emotions which are different, and divide. What then was it that was so very original? Rousseau's name is, of course, associated with the *Social Contract*, but there is nothing new in that either. The notion that men in society, in order to preserve themselves, have had historically to enter some kind of compact; or if not historically, at any rate that they behave as if they had done so; that men in society, because some are stronger than others, or more malevolent than others, have had to set up institutions whereby the weak majority is able to prevent the strong minority from riding roughshod over them – that is an idea certainly as old as the Greeks.

What, then, is it, apart from minor variations, that Rousseau added to this theme? Some might say he effected a reconciliation between individual liberty and the authority of the community. But this was one question which had been discussed times out of number by his predecessors. Indeed, the central question which occupied thinkers like Machiavelli and Bodin, Hobbes and Locke, was this very question. Nothing is more familiar or more natural in the history of political thought than the question 'How is men's desire for liberty to be reconciled with the need for authority?' It is clear to all political thinkers that individuals wish to be free – that is to say, they wish to do whatever they wish to do, without being prevented from doing it by other people, or coerced into doing something they do not want to do – and that this freedom from coercion is one of the chief ends or values for the sake of which people are prepared to fight, one of the ends whose realisation is indispensable for leading the kind of life which most men wish to lead.

On the other hand, of course, there is the necessity for organised existence. Men do live in society, for whatever cause or reason; and because men live in society, individuals cannot be allowed to do whatever they like, because this may get in the way of other people, and frustrate their ends too much. Therefore some kind of social arrangement has to be made.

Among earlier thinkers this very central problem had led to various answers. It led to answers which varied in accordance with the view of the human individual taken by these different thinkers. Hobbes, who took a somewhat low view of human nature and thought that man on the whole was bad rather than good, savage rather than tame, thought that strong authority was necessary in order to curb the naturally wild, unruly and bestial impulses of man; and therefore drew the frontier between authority and liberty in favour of authority. He thought that a good deal of coercion was needed to prevent human beings from destroying each other, from ruining each other's lives, from creating conditions in which life would be perilous, nasty, brutish and short for the vast majority of society. Therefore he left the area for individual liberty rather small.

Locke, on the other hand, who believed that men were good more than wicked, thought that it was not necessary to draw the frontier quite so far in favour of authority, and held that it was possible to create a society in which some of those rights which, according to him, men possessed before they entered into societies – while they were in the 'state of nature' – were still retained by them even in civil society; and allowed men a good many more individual rights than Hobbes did, on the ground that they were more benevolent by nature, and that it was not necessary to crush them, coerce them and restrain them to quite the severe degree demanded by Hobbes in order to create that minimum of security which alone enables society to survive.

But the point I wish to make is that the argument between them is simply an argument about where the frontier is to be drawn, and the frontier is a shifting one. In the Middle Ages, when political thought was largely theological, this took the form of disagreement about whether original sin, which made man wild, wicked, voracious and unruly, was something stronger in him than natural or God-given reason, which made him seek after good and proper ends, implanted in him by God. In more secular ages, when these concepts became insensibly translated into secular terms, the same argument as to where the frontier was to be drawn took a more secular historical or psychological form. The question now was: 'How much liberty and how much authority? How much coercion versus how much individual freedom?' Some compromise had to be reached: and you simply arrived at the solution – at the estimation of where the frontier must be drawn – in accordance with what seemed to you to be the true constitution of human nature, in the light of, perhaps, such scientific data as the influence of climate, of environment, and other similar factors, which a thinker like Montesquieu, for example, takes into such great consideration.

The original aspect of Rousseau's teaching is that this entire approach will not do at all. His notion of liberty and his notion of authority are very different from those of previous thinkers, and although he uses the same words, he puts into them a very different content. This, indeed, may be one of the great secrets of his eloquence and of his immense effectiveness, namely that, while he appears to be saying things not very different from his predecessors, using the same kinds of sentences, and apparently the same concepts, yet he alters the meanings of the words, he twists the concepts in such a fashion that they produce an electrifying effect upon the reader, who is insensibly drawn by the familiar expressions into wholly unfamiliar country.

Rousseau says one thing and conveys another. He appears to be arguing along old-fashioned lines, but the vision which he projects before the reader is something totally unlike the schema which he appears to borrow from his predecessors. Let us take, for example, such central concepts in his teaching as the notion of liberty, the notion of contract, the notion of nature.

First, liberty. For Rousseau the whole idea of compromising liberty, of saying 'Well now, we cannot have total liberty, because that will lead to anarchy and chaos; we cannot have complete authority, because that will lead to the total crushing of individuals, despotism and tyranny; therefore we must draw the line somewhere between, arrange a compromise' – this kind of thinking is totally unacceptable. Liberty for him is an absolute value. He looks on liberty as if it were a kind of religious concept. For him, liberty is identical with the human individual himself. To say that a man is a man, and to say that he is free, are almost the same.

What is a man for Rousseau? A man is somebody responsible for his acts – capable of doing good and evil, capable of following the path either of right or of wrong. If he is not free, this distinction becomes meaningless. If a man is not free, if a man is not responsible for what he does, if a man does not do what he does because he wants to do it, because this is his personal, human goal, because in this way he achieves something which he, and not somebody else, at this moment desires – if he does not do that, he is not a human being at all: for he has no accountability. The whole notion of moral responsibility, which for Rousseau is the essence of man almost more than his reason, depends upon the fact that a man can choose, choose between alternatives, choose between them freely, be uncoerced.

If a man is coerced, coerced by somebody else, by a tyrant, or even by material circumstances, then it is absurd to say that he chooses; for Rousseau he becomes a thing, a chattel, an object in nature, something from which no accountability can be expected. Tables and chairs, and even animals, cannot be regarded as doing right and wrong, for they either do not do anything, or know not what they do, and if they do not know they cannot be said to act; and not to act is not to be a human being. Action is choosing, choosing implies selection between alternative goals. Someone who cannot choose between alternative goals because he is compelled is to that extent not human. This would be the case if he is an object determined in nature, as the physicists had taught, simply a bundle of nerves and blood and bones, a collection of atoms, as much under the sway of material laws as the inanimate objects of nature. Alternatively, if he is determined not as things are determined in nature, but in another way – because he is bullied or coerced by a tyrant, because he is made the creature of somebody else who plays upon his fears, or his hopes, or his vanity, and is manipulated like a puppet – a creature like that is equally not fully capable of freedom, not fully capable of action, and is therefore not fully a human being.

There is no saying but what a man in this condition – for Rousseau, a slave – might not be happy, but happiness is not the goal of men: the goal is to live the right kind of life. Therefore, for Rousseau, the proposition that slaves may often be happier than free men does not begin to justify slavery, and for this reason he sharply and indignantly rejects the utilitarianism of people like Helvétius. Slavery may be a source of happiness: but it is monstrous all the same. For man to wish to be a slave may be prudent, but it is disgusting, detestably degrading. For 'slavery . . . is against nature', and the unanimity of servitude is quite different from the unanimity of a genuine assembly of men. 'To renounce liberty', declares Rousseau, 'is to renounce being a man, to surrender the rights of humanity, and even its duties ... Such a renunciation is not compatible with man's nature.'

This means that for a man to lose his liberty is for him to cease to be a man, and that is why a man cannot sell himself into slavery, for once he becomes a slave, he is no longer a man, and therefore has no rights, no duties, and a man cannot cancel himself out, he cannot commit an act whose consequence is that he can commit no further acts. To do this is to commit moral suicide, and suicide is not a human action – 'death is not an event in life'. Liberty, therefore, for Rousseau, is not something which can be adjusted or compromised: you are not allowed to give away now a little of it, now much more of it; you are not allowed to barter so much freedom for so much security, so much freedom for so much happiness. To yield 'a little' of your liberty is like dying a little, dehumanising yourself a little; and the belief which is most passionately held by Rousseau, one of the values to which he devoted more eloquence than to almost any other, is this notion of human integrity, the fact that the ultimate crime, the one sin not to be borne, is dehumanisation of man, degradation and exploitation of man. He spends a great deal of his passionate rhetoric on denouncing those who use other people for their own selfish purposes – not because they make the people whom they use unhappy, but because they deform them, they make them lose their human semblance. That is, for him, the sin against the Holy Ghost. In short, human freedom – the capacity to choose ends independently, auto-nomously – is for Rousseau an absolute value, and to say of a value that it is absolute is to say that one cannot compromise over it at all.

So far so good. Rousseau has made clear that his attitude towards man entails regarding liberty as the most sacred of human attributes – indeed not as an attribute at all, but as the essence of what being a man is. But there are other values too. It is impossible simply to declare that freedom, individual freedom, permission for men to do what they like, a situation in which anybody does anything, is the ideal condition of man. This is for two reasons. In the first place there is the empirical or historical reason. For one reason or another, for one cause or another, men do live in societies. Why this happens, Rousseau never quite clearly explains. Possibly it is because of the inequality of gifts, which makes some men stronger than others, and enables them to assert their power over others, and so enslave them. Perhaps also because of some inevitable law of social evolution, perhaps because of some natural instinct of sociableness which drives people to live together. Perhaps, again, for some such reasons as those which the Encyclopaedists spoke of: division of labour and co-operation for the purpose of leading a life which satisfies a greater number of human wishes, and the wishes of more individuals, than the isolated life of savages could satisfy.

Sometimes Rousseau talks about the savage as if he was happy, innocent and good; at other times as if he was merely simple and barbarous. But be that as it may, men do live in society, and consequently have to create rules whereby human beings must so conduct themselves as not to get in each other's way too much, not frustrate each other excessively, not employ their power in such a way as to thwart too many of each other's purposes and ends. So now we are faced with the problem: How is a human being to remain absolutely free (for if he is not free, he is not human), and yet not be allowed to do absolutely everything he wants? Yet if he is stopped, how can he be free? For what is freedom, if it is not doing what he wants, and not being stopped from doing it?

Secondly, there is also for Rousseau a further and a deeper reason for coercion. Rousseau was, after all, a citizen of Geneva, and deeply affected by its Calvinist traditions; and therefore, for him, there is an ever-present vision of the rules of life. He is deeply concerned about right and wrong, about justice and injustice. There are certain ways of living which are right, and certain ways of living which are wrong. In common with the rest of the eighteenth century he believes that the question 'How should I live?' is a real question; and therefore, however we may come by it, by reason, or by some other route, that there is some answer to it.

Given that I have obtained this answer – or that I think I have obtained it – it will take the form of rules of life which, in effect, say 'Do thus: do not do thus', or statements of the form 'This is wrong: this is right. This is just: this is unjust. This is good: this is bad. This is handsome: this is ugly.' But once we have rules, once we have laws, principles, canons, once we have some kind of regulations which prescribe conduct, what is to happen to liberty? How can liberty be compatible with regulations, which after all hem man in, prevent him from doing absolutely anything he wants, tell him what to do and what not to do, forbid him to do certain things, control him to a certain degree?

Rousseau is very passionate about this. He says that these laws, these rules of life, are not conventions; they are not utilitarian devices invented by man simply for the purpose of achieving some short-term, or even long-term, subjective purpose. Not at all. Let me quote from him again. He speaks of 'the law of nature, the sacred imprescriptible law which speaks to the heart of man and to his reason', and says that it is 'graven on the hearts of men better than all the rubbish of Justinian'. The power of willing or of choosing the right path, he claims, is not explicable by any mechanical laws. It is something inherent in man, and the subject-matter of no natural science. The moral laws which man obeys are absolute, something from which man knows that he must not depart. In this respect Rousseau's view is a secular version of Calvinism, for the one thing which he perpetually insists upon is that laws are not conventions, are not utilitarian devices, but simply the drawing up in terms suitable to the particular time and place and people of regulations embodying sacred truths, sacred rules which are not man-made, but eternal, universal and absolute.

So we have a paradox. We have two absolute values: the absolute value of freedom and the absolute value of the right rules. And we are not allowed to compromise between them. We are not allowed to do what Hobbes thought might be done, namely to establish a *de facto* regime allowing so much freedom, so much authority, so much control, so much individual initiative. Neither of the absolute values may be derogated from: to derogate from freedom is to kill man's immortal soul; to derogate from the rules is to permit something absolutely wrong, absolutely bad, absolutely wicked, to fly against the sacred source of the rules, called sometimes nature, sometimes conscience, sometimes God – but which in any case is absolute. This is the dilemma in which Rousseau is plunged, and it is very different from the problem of those previous thinkers who believed in adjustment, in compromise, in empirical devices as means for finding a solution which would of course not be ideal, but adequate; neither wholly good nor wholly evil, but more good than evil; something enabling human beings to carry on not too badly, reasonably well; something based upon common sense and due respect, moderate, decent respect for most of each other's wishes, so that people on the whole get, not indeed all they want, but protection for minimal 'rights', and more than they would get under some other system. This kind of outlook, typical of Hobbes and Locke, Helvétius and Mill, is for Rousseau totally unacceptable. An absolute value means that you cannot compromise, you cannot modify; and he puts this in a very dramatic fashion. He says that the problem for him is 'to find a form of association ... in which each, while uniting himself with all, yet may still obey only himself alone and remain as free as before'.

This certainly puts the paradox in an appropriately paradoxical form. How can we at one and the same time unite ourselves with other people, and therefore found a form of association which must exercise some degree of authority, of coercion – very different from being entirely free or solitary in a state of nature – and yet remain free, that is, not obey these same people?

Rousseau's world-famous answer was given by him in the *Social Contract*, and it is that each man, 'in giving himself to all, gives himself to nobody'. This celebrated formula, evocative as it is, is as dark and mysterious now as it ever was. Rousseau loved paradox, but his strangeness as a thinker goes deeper than that. He was obviously deeply tormented by the dilemma of freedom versus moral authority, on neither horn of which he wished to impale himself. Then suddenly there came to him a blinding solution to it. In a letter to Malesherbes he gives a vivid account of how one such revolution dawned upon him. He was on his

revelation

way to visit his friend Diderot in prison when the solution of the problem of human vice and virtue came upon him with a blinding flash of inspiration. He felt like a mathematician who had suddenly solved a long and torturing problem, like an artist to whom a vision had suddenly been vouchsafed, like a mystic who had suddenly seen the truth, the transcendental beatific truth itself. He tells us how he sat down at the roadside and wept and was beside himself, and how this was the central event of his entire life. The tone in which he communicates the answers to the ancient puzzles, both in the *Social Contract* and in other works, is exactly that of a man possessed by a single idea, of a maniac who suddenly sees a cosmic solution vouchsafed to him alone, somebody who for the first time in history has suddenly found the answer to a riddle which had for centuries tormented the whole of humanity, which previous great thinkers, perhaps Plato, perhaps the founder of Christianity, had in some degree anticipated, but which he and he alone had at last found in its full richness, so that nobody need trouble to look for the solution again.

He is, at such moments, like a mad mathematician who has found a solution which is not merely true, but demonstrable, by rules of such iron logic that nobody will ever reopen the question. What is this solution? Rousseau proceeds like a geometer, with two lines which intersect each other at one point and one only. He says to himself: 'Here is liberty and here is authority, and it is difficult – it is logically impossible – to arrange a compromise. How are we to reconcile them?' The answer has a kind of simplicity and a kind of lunacy which maniacal natures are often capable of. There is no question of compromise. The problem must be viewed in such a way that one suddenly perceives that, so far from being incompatible, the two opposed values are not opposed at all, not two at all, but one. Liberty and authority cannot conflict for they are *one*; they coincide; they are the reverse and obverse of the same medal. There is a liberty which is identical with authority; and it is possible to have a personal freedom which is the same as complete control by authority. The more free you are, the more authority you have, and also the more you obey; the more liberty, the more control.

How is this mysterious point of intersection to be achieved? Rousseau's solution is that, after all, freedom simply consists in men wanting certain things and not being prevented from having them. What, then, do they want? What I necessarily want is that which is good for me – that which alone will satisfy my nature. Of course, if I do not know what is good for me, then when I get what I want, I suffer, because it turns out not to be what I had really wanted at all. Therefore those alone are free who not merely want certain things but also know what, in fact, will alone satisfy them.

If a man knows what will satisfy him, then he is endowed with reason; and reason gives him the answer to the question: 'What should I seek for in order that I may be – that my nature may be – fully satisfied?' What is true for one rational man will be true for other rational men, just as, in the case of the sciences, what one scientist finds to be true will be accepted by other scientists; so that if you have reached your conclusion by a valid method from true premises, using correct rules, you may be certain that other people, if they are rational, will arrive at the same solution; or alternatively, if you feel sure of the rationality of your thought, but they arrive at some different solution, this alone shows you that they cannot possibly be rational; and you may safely ignore their conclusions.

Rousseau knows that, since nature is a harmony (and this is the great premiss, the great and dubious premiss of almost all of eighteenth-century thought), it follows that what I truly want cannot collide with what somebody else truly wants. For the good is what will truly satisfy anyone's rational demands; and if it were the case that what I truly want does not tally with what somebody else truly, in other words rationally, wants, then two true answers to two genuine questions will be incompatible with each other; and that is logically impossible. For that would mean that nature is not a harmony, that tragedy is inevitable, that conflict cannot be avoided, that somewhere in the heart of things there is something irrational, that do what I may, be I never so wise, whatever weapons of reason I employ, however good I am, however upright, however clear-headed and reasonable and profound and wise, I may yet want something when an equally wise, equally good and virtuous man may wish the opposite of it. There will be nothing to choose between us: no criterion of morality, no principle of justice, divine or human. Therefore tragedy will turn out, after all, to be due not to human error, human stupidity and human mistakes, but to a flaw in the universe; and that conclusion neither Rousseau nor any other prominent eighteenth-century thinker, with the exception, perhaps, of the Marquis de Sade, accepts. But Sade was a notoriously vicious madman, and when Voltaire and Hume hinted at something of the kind, this was put down to the cynicism of the one and the scepticism of the other, in neither case to be taken too seriously; indeed neither Voltaire nor Hume were any too anxious to stress this aspect of their thought.

Consequently, if nature is a harmony, then anything which satisfies one rational man must be of such a kind as to be compatible, at any rate, with whatever satisfies other rational men. Rousseau argues that all that is necessary is for men not to seek the kind of ends which conflict with the ends of others. Why do they now tend to seek such ends? Because they are corrupt, because they are not rational, because they are not natural; and this concept of nature in Rousseau, although in certain respects like the concept of nature in other thinkers, nevertheless acquires a tone of its own. Rousseau is sure that he knows what it is to be a natural man: to him to be natural is to be good, and if all men were natural, they would all be good; what they would then seek would be something which would make each and all of them satisfied, taken together, as a single harmonious whole. For the unanimity of rational beings, willing rational ends which, *ex hypothesi*, are one single end, though willed by many individual wills, is a very singular affair. Let me quote him again: 'As long as several men in the assembly regard themselves as a single body they have only a single will ... The constant willing of all the members of the State is the general will.' This 'general will' is something that 'penetrates into a man's innermost being, and concerns itself with his will no less than with his actions'.

We may well, at this point, ask what this general will is. What is there about these men in the assembly that generates something which can be called a single will which holds for them all? Rousseau's answer is that, just as all men who argue rationally reach the same truth about matters of fact (politics and morals apart), and these truths are always necessarily compatible, so men in the same condition of nature – that is to say, unperverted, uncorrupted, not pulled at by selfish interests, not pulled at by regional or sectional interests, not enslaved by fear or by unworthy hopes, men not bullied, not twisted out of their proper nature by the wickedness of other men – men in that condition must want that which, if it is obtained, will be equally good for all other men who are as good as they are. Therefore, so long as we are able somehow or other to regain, to recapture what is for him the original innocent state of nature in which men were not yet prey to the many passions, to the many wicked and evil impulses, which civilisation has bred in the human breast, natural harmony, happiness and goodness will once more be the lot of human society.

Rousseau's notion of the natural man was, naturally, affected by the kind of man he was. Rousseau was a *petit bourgeois* from Geneva who lived his early life as a tramp, and who was at odds with the society of his time, and was the prey of many kinds of what nowadays are called inferiority complexes. Consequently his notion of a natural man is the idealised opposite of the kind of persons whom he particularly detested and disliked. He denounces not merely the rich, not merely the powerful: few moralists have failed to regard these two classes as the natural enemies of society. He denounced, and is almost the first to denounce, a very different set of persons, and by this means deeply affected the consciousness of the next century. For all that he was a composer and a musical theorist, he detested the arts and the sciences; he disliked every form of sophistication, every form of refinement, every form of fastidiousness. He is the first person to say quite explicitly and openly that the good man is not merely simple, not merely poor – sentiments which many a Christian thinker has held – he goes further and thinks that the rough is better than the smooth, the savage better than the tame, the disturbed better than the tranquil. Rousseau is filled with deep resentment of cliques, of coteries, of sets; above all he suffers from a deep resentment of intellectuals, of those who take pride in cleverness, of experts or specialists who set themselves up over the heads of the people. All those nineteenth-century thinkers who are violently anti-intellectual, and in a sense anti-cultural, indeed the aggressive philistines of the next two centuries – whom Nietzsche called *Kulturphilister* – including Nietzsche himself, are the natural descendants of Rousseau.

Rousseau's tormented and tortured nature made him look with eyes of hatred upon people like Diderot, d'Alembert, Helvétius in Paris, who seemed to him fastidious, sophisticated and artificial, incapable of understanding all those dark emotions, all those deep and torturing feelings which ravaged the heart of a true natural man torn from his native soil. The natural man, for him, was somebody who possessed a deep instinctive wisdom very different from the corrupt sophistication of the towns. Rousseau is the greatest militant lowbrow of history, a kind of guttersnipe of genius, and figures like Carlyle, and to some extent Nietzsche, and certainly D. H. Lawrence and d'Annunzio, as well as *révolté*, *petit bourgeois* dictators like Hitler and Mussolini, are his heirs.

It is difficult, and indeed gratuitous, to classify this as a right-wing or a left-wing phenomenon. It is mainly a kind of *petit bourgeois* revolt against a society from which the *déclassé* feels excluded. Rousseau makes common cause with the outcasts, the rebels, the free wild artists. That is what makes him the founder of romanticism and wild individualism, as well as the founder of so many other movements of the nineteenth century – of socialism and communism, of authoritarianism and nationalism, of democratic liberalism and anarchism, of almost everything, save what might be called liberal civilisation, with its fastidious love of culture, in the two centuries which followed publication of the *Social Contract*.

Rousseau hates intellectuals, hates persons who detach themselves from life, hates specialists, hates people who lock themselves up into some kind of special coterie, because he feels that hearts ought to be opened, so that men may achieve emotional contact; that the simple peasant sitting under the ancestral oak has a deeper vision of what life is like, and what nature is like, and what conduct ought to be, than the buttoned-up, priggish, fastidious, sophisticated, highbrow person who lives in the city. Because he feels all that, he founds a tradition distinct from that of the romantic rebel, which then spreads all over Europe, and then to the United States, and is the foundation of that celebrated concept called the American way of life, in accordance with which the simple people of a society possess a deeper sense of reality, a deeper virtue and a deeper understanding of moral values than professors in their universities, than the politicians of the cities, than other people who have somehow become de-natured, who have somehow cut themselves off from the inner stream which is at once the true life and the true morality and wisdom of men and societies.

That is the kind of impression which Rousseau communicates when he talks about nature, and although we are told that there are at least sixty senses in which the word 'nature' is used in the eighteenth century, Rousseau's usage is unique. He goes further than anybody in identifying nature not merely with simplicity, but with a genuine loathing of civilised, elaborate, sophisticated artistic or scientific values. Neither artists nor scientists must guide society – that is why he dislikes Helvétius and the Encyclopaedists so acutely. Society must be led by the man who is in touch with the truth, and the man who is in touch with the truth is somebody who allows this divine grace, who allows the truth which nature alone possesses, to pour into his heart. This may be done only in the bosom of nature, only if we live the simple life. At first the simple life in Rousseau is merely a description of the kind of conditions in which the true answer may be vouchsafed. To those who crave for it, gradually it becomes that truth itself: it becomes difficult to distinguish, both in *Émile* and *La Nouvelle Héloïse*, between the conditions for knowing the answers to questions, and the answers themselves. For Rousseau, ultimately, the answer resides in being a certain kind of person: in having one's heart in the right place. To have a certain kind of knowledge – that is the key to all the problems.

In theory Rousseau speaks like any other eighteenth-century *philosophe*, and says: 'We must employ our reason.' He uses deductive reasoning, sometimes very cogent, very lucid and extremely well-expressed, for reaching his conclusions. But in reality what happens is that this deductive reasoning is like a strait-jacket of logic which he claps upon the inner, burning, almost lunatic vision within; it is this extraordinary combination of the insane inner vision with the cold rigorous strait-jacket of a kind of Calvinistic logic which really gives his prose its powerful enchantment and its hypnotic effect. You appear to be reading logical argument which distinguishes between concepts and draws conclusions in a valid manner from premises, when all the time something very violent is being said to you. A vision is being imposed on you; somebody is trying to dominate you by means of a very coherent, although often a very deranged, vision of life, to bind a spell, not to argue, despite the cool and collected way in which he appears to be talking.

The inner vision is the mysterious assumption of the coincidence of authority and liberty. The coincidence itself derives from the fact that, in order to make men at once free and capable of living with each other in society, and of obeying the moral law, what you want is that men shall want only that which the moral law in fact enjoins. In short, the problem goes somewhat as follows. You want to give people unlimited liberty because otherwise they cease to be men; and yet at the same time you want them to live according to the rules. If they can be made to love the rules, then they will want the rules, not so much because the rules are rules as because they love them. If your problem is how a man shall be at once free and yet in chains, you say: 'What if the chains are not imposed upon him? What if the chains are not something with which he is bound as by some external force? What if the chains are something he chooses himself because such a choice is an expression of his nature, something he generates from within him as an inner ideal? If this is what he above all wants in the world, then the chains are no longer chains.' A man who is self-chained is not a prisoner. So Rousseau says: 'Man is born free, and yet he is everywhere in

chains.' What sort of chains? If they are the chains of convention, if they are the chains of the tyrant, if they are the chains of
other people who want to use you for their own ends, then these
are indeed chains, and you must fight and you must struggle,
and nothing must stand in the way of the great battle for
individual self-assertion and freedom. But if the chains are
chains of your own making, if the chains are simply the rules
which you forge, with your own inner reason, or because of the
grace which pours in while you lead the simple life, or because
of the voice of conscience or the voice of God or the voice of
nature, which are all referred to by Rousseau as if they were
almost the same thing; if the chains are simply rules the very
obedience to which is the most free, the strongest, most
spontaneous expression of your own inner nature, then the
chains no longer bind you – since self-control is not control.
Self-control is freedom. In this way Rousseau gradually pro-
gresses towards the peculiar idea that what is wanted is men who
want to be connected with each other in the way in which the
State forcibly connects them.

The original chains are some form of coercion which the
tyrant used to employ in order to force you to do his will, and it
is this which poets have so wickedly embellished with their
garlands; it is this which writers have so fulsomely and so
immorally tried to camouflage by the encomia which they have
paid to mere force, to mere authority. But what is wanted is
something very different. What is wanted – I quote Rousseau
again – is 'the surrender of each individual with all his rights to
the whole community'. If you surrender yourself to the whole
community, then how can you not be free, for who coerces you?
Not X, not Y, not this or that institution – it is the State which
coerces you. But what is the State? The State is you, and others
like you, all seeking your common good. For Rousseau there
does exist a common good, for if there were not something
which is the common good of the whole society, which does not
conflict with individual goods, then to ask 'How shall we live?
What shall we, a group of men together, do?' would be senseless,
and that is patently absurd.

Consequently Rousseau develops the notion of the general

will. It begins in the harmless notion of a contract, which after all is a semi-commercial affair, merely a kind of undertaking voluntarily entered into, and ultimately revocable also, an act performed by human beings who come together and agree to do certain things intended to lead to their common happiness; but still only an arrangement of convenience which, if it leads to common misery, they can abandon. This is how it begins; but from the notion of a social contract as a perfectly voluntary act on the part of individuals who remain individual and who pursue each his own good, Rousseau gradually moves towards the notion of the general will as almost the personified willing of a large super-personal entity, of something called 'the State', which is now no longer the crushing leviathan of Hobbes, but something rather more like a team, something like a Church, a unity in diversity, a greater-than-I, something in which I sink my personality only in order to find it again.

There is a mystical moment in which Rousseau mysteriously passes from the notion of a group of individuals in voluntary, free relations with each other, each pursuing his own good, to the notion of submission to something which is myself, and yet greater than myself – the whole, the community. The steps by which he reaches it are peculiar and worth examining briefly.

I say to myself that there are certain things which I desire, and if I am stopped from having them, then I am not free; and this is the worst thing which can befall me. I then say to myself, 'What is it that I desire?' I desire only the satisfaction of my nature. If I am wise, and if I am rational, well-informed, clear-sighted, then I discover in what this satisfaction lies. The true satisfaction of any one man cannot clash with the true satisfaction of any other man, for if it clashed, nature would not be harmonious and one truth would collide with another, which is logically impossible. I may find that other men are trying to frustrate me. Why are they doing this? If I know that I am right, if I know that what I seek is the true good, then people who oppose me must be in error about what it is that they themselves seek. No doubt they too think that they are seeking the good, they assert their own liberty to secure it, but they are seeking it in the wrong place. Therefore I have a right to prevent them. In virtue of what have

I this right to prevent them? Not because I want something that they do not want, not because I am superior to them, not because I am stronger than they are, not even because I am wiser than they are, for they are human beings with immortal souls, and as such my equals, and Rousseau passionately believes in equality. It is because, if they knew what they truly wanted, they would seek what I seek. The fact that they do not seek this means that they do not *really* know – and it is 'truly' and 'really' which, as so often, are the treacherous words.

What Rousseau really wishes to convey is that every man is potentially good – nobody can be altogether bad. If men allowed their natural goodness to well out from them, then they would want only what is right; and the fact that they do not want it merely means that they do not understand their own nature. But the nature is there, for all that. For Rousseau, to say that a man wants what is bad, although potentially he wants what is good, is like saying that there is some secret part of himself which is his 'real' self; that if he were *himself*, if he were as he ought to be, if he were his true self, then he would seek the good. From that it is but a small step to saying that there is a sense in which he already seeks this good, but does not know this. It is true that if you ask him what it is that he wants, he may enunciate some very evil purpose. But the true man inside him, the immortal soul, that which would speak out if only he allowed nature to penetrate his breast, if only he lived the right kind of life, and viewed himself as he really is, his true self, seeks something else.

I know what any man's true self seeks; for it must seek what my own self seeks, whenever I know that what I am now is my own true self, and not my other, illusory, self. It is this notion of the two selves which really does the work in Rousseau's thought. When I stop a man from pursuing evil ends, even when I put him in jail in order to prevent him from causing damage to other good men, even if I execute him as an abandoned criminal, I do this not for utilitarian reasons, in order to give happiness to others; not even for retributive reasons, in order to punish him for the evil that he does. I do it because that is what his own inner, better, more real self would have done if only he had allowed it to speak. I set myself up as the authority not merely

46

over my actions, but over his. This is what is meant by Rousseau's famous phrase about the right of society to force men to be free.

To force a man to be free is to force him to behave in a rational manner. A man is free who gets what he wants; what he truly wants is a rational end. If he does not want a rational end, he does not truly want; if he does not want a rational end, what he wants is not true freedom but false freedom. I force him to do certain things which will make him happy. He will be grateful to me for it if he ever discovers what his own true self is: that is the heart of this famous doctrine, and there is not a dictator in the West who in the years after Rousseau did not use this monstrous paradox in order to justify his behaviour. The Jacobins, Robespierre, Hitler, Mussolini, the Communists all use this very same method of argument, of saying men do not know what they truly want – and therefore by wanting it for them, by wanting it on their behalf, we are giving them what in some occult sense, without knowing it themselves, they themselves 'really' want. When I execute the criminal, when I bend human beings to my will, even when I organise inquisitions, when I torture men and kill them, I am not merely doing something which is good for them – though even that is quite dubious enough – I am doing that which they truly want, though they may deny it a thousand times. If they do deny it, that is because they do not know what they are, what they want, what the world is like. Therefore I speak for them, on their behalf. This is Rousseau's central doctrine, and it is a doctrine which leads to genuine servitude, and by this route, from this deification of the notion of absolute liberty, we gradually reach the notion of absolute despotism. There is no reason why human beings should be offered choices, alternatives, when only one alternative is the right alternative. Certainly they must choose, because if they do not choose then they are not spontaneous, they are not free, they are not human beings; but if they do not choose the right alternative, if they choose the wrong alternative, it is because their true self is not at work. They do not know what their true self is, whereas I, who am wise, who am rational, who am the great benevolent legislator – I know this. Rousseau, who had democratic instincts, leaned not so much towards individual legislators as towards assemblies, assemblies which, however, were only right to the extent to which they resolved to do that which the reason inside all the members of the assembly, their true self, genuinely desired.

It is in virtue of this doctrine that Rousseau lives as a political thinker. The doctrine did both evil and good. Good in the sense that he stressed the fact that without freedom, without spontaneity, no society is worth having, that a society as conceived by the utilitarians of the eighteenth century, in which a few experts organised life in a sleek and frictionless manner, so as to endow the largest number of people with as much happiness as possible, is repulsive to a human being, who prefers wild, unruly, spontaneous freedom, provided that it is he himself who is acting; prefers this even to the maximum of happiness if that results from being worked into an artificial system, not by his own will, but by the will of some superior specialist, some manager, some arranger of society in a set pattern.

The evil that Rousseau did consists in launching the mythology of the real self, in the name of which I am permitted to coerce people. No doubt all inquisitors, and all the great religious establishments, sought to justify their acts of coercion, which subsequently may have appeared, to some people at any rate, cruel and unjust; but at least they invoked supernatural sanctions for them. At least they invoked sanctions which reason was not allowed to question. But Rousseau believed that everything could be discovered by mere untrammelled human reason, by mere unobstructed observation of nature, of actual three-dimensional nature, of nature simply in the sense of objects in space – human beings and animals and inanimate objects. Lacking the aid of supernatural authority, he therefore had to resort to the monstrous paradox whereby liberty turns out to be a kind of slavery, whereby to want something is not to want it at all unless you want it in a special way, such that you can say to a man: 'You may think that you are free, you may think that you are happy, you may think that you want this or that, but I know better what you are, what you want, what will liberate you', and so on. This is the sinister paradox according to

48

which a man, in losing his political liberty, and in losing his economic liberty, is liberated in some higher, deeper, more rational, more natural sense, which only the dictator or only the State, only the assembly, only the supreme authority knows, so that the most untrammelled freedom coincides with the most rigorous and enslaving authority.

For this great perversion Rousseau is more responsible than any thinker who ever lived. The consequences of it in the nineteenth and twentieth centuries need not be enlarged upon – they are still with us. In that sense it is not in the least paradoxical to say that Rousseau, who claims to have been the most ardent and passionate lover of human liberty who ever lived, who tried to throw off every shackle, the restraints of education, of sophistication, of culture, of convention, of science, of art, of everything whatever, because all these things somehow impinged upon him, all these things in some way arrested his natural liberty as a man – Rousseau, in spite of all these things, was one of the most sinister and most formidable enemies of liberty in the whole history of modern thought.

FICHTE

MORE THAN ANY OTHER German thinker, Johann Gottlieb
Fichte appears to me to be responsible for launching an idea of
freedom which is in sharp contrast and disagreement with that
notion of freedom or liberty normally held by Western – that is
to say, principally English, French and American – thinkers in
the late eighteenth century and the nineteenth century.

Suppose that you were travelling about Europe at some time
between the years 1800 and 1820. You would have discovered,
to your surprise, that although the word 'freedom' was on every
lip from the East to the West – although, if anything, the
Germans and Austrians talked about it with more passion and
eloquence even than people in France and in England – yet the
meaning attached to the word differed widely between the two
parts of Europe. It bore a very different sense in Germany from
that which it appeared to have for thinkers in the great Anglo-
French tradition.

What does 'freedom' mean for the principal political writers
of the West at this time, for Condorcet, say, for Tom Paine, for
Benjamin Constant – three representative thinkers, all of whom
felt passionately on this subject, and all writers whose ideas had
a very considerable influence both on contemporaries and on
posterity? Let me quote a specimen passage from Constant, a
very moderate, sensible liberal whose political writings belong to
the beginning of the nineteenth century and who spoke for a
large body of liberal democrats of his time. In a lecture delivered
in 1819, in which he compares what he calls the modern with the
ancient notion of liberty, he asks what his contemporaries mean
by 'liberty'. This is his definition:

It is the individual's right to be subject only to law, his right not to be arrested or detained or put to death or maltreated in any way as the result of the arbitrary will of one or several persons. It is every man's right to express his opinion, to choose his craft and exercise it, to dispose of his property, even to misuse it if he wishes; to come and go without getting permission for it, and without having to give any account of his reasons or motives. It is each man's right to associate himself with others, whether to discuss his own interests or to profess his religion, if he wishes, with his associates, or simply to pass his days and hours in any manner that accords with his inclination or his fancy. Finally it is everyone's right to influence the conduct of the government whether by nominating some or all of its public servants, or by representations, petitions, demands, which the authorities are more or less compelled to take into its consideration.

Then he adds that in the ancient world it was not so; there, although in some sense the individual was sovereign in public affairs, he was much more controlled and restricted in his private life; whereas in modern States, even in democratic States, the individual seemed comparatively powerless to influence the decisions of the political authorities; and fought precisely for this right.

That is a fair sample of what the word 'liberty' meant to moderate defenders of it in the early nineteenth century. But you would find that it was very different in the Germany of this period.

Fichte was always saying that liberty was the only subject with which he was at all concerned. 'My system, from beginning to end, is merely an analysis of the concept of freedom . . . no other ingredient enters into it.' Then he warns the reader – and warns him very clearly – by insisting that his doctrine is very dark, and the language is not to be understood by ordinary men; that a special act of transformation or conversion or illumination is needed before the deep significance of his inspired utterance can be understood at all.

To men [Fichte declares] as they are in their ordinary education, our philosophical theory must be absolutely unintelligible, for the object of which it speaks does not exist for them; they do not possess that special faculty for which, and by which, alone this object has any being. It is as if one were talking to men blind from birth; men who know things and their relations only by touch, and one spoke to them about colours and the relations of colours.

The reason why it is so unintelligible to ordinary men is that they are not endowed with the special, profoundly metaphysical faculty of perceiving such invaluable truths, which are open only to a very few men in each generation. Fichte regards himself as one of these few. His grasp of the essence of freedom is due to this special penetration into the nature of the universe. Let me explain this a little further.

The principal preoccupation of many Western European thinkers was to guard the liberty of the individual against encroachment by other individuals. What they meant by liberty was non-interference – a fundamentally negative concept. Treated in that way, it is the subject of the great classical thesis – the essay on liberty by John Stuart Mill, which to this day remains the most eloquent, the most sincere and the most convincing plea for individual freedom ever uttered.

This is what liberty meant to Condorcet. This is what it meant to the majority of those French rebels who raised revolutionary standards in order to liberate the individual, and then sent their armies across Europe in order to liberate other nations. The assumption is that each individual has certain tastes, certain desires, certain inclinations, and wishes to lead his life in a certain fashion. Certainly he cannot be allowed to do so wholly, because if he does he will interfere too much with the similar ends of others. But a certain vacuum round him has to be created, a certain space within which he may be allowed to fulfil what might be called his reasonable wishes. One should not criticise these wishes. Each man's ends are his own; the business of the State is to prevent collisions; to act as a kind of traffic policeman and night-watchman, as the German socialist Lassalle contemptuously observed later in the century; simply to see to it that people do not clash with each other too much in the fulfilling of those personal ends about which they themselves are the ultimate authorities. Liberty means non-encroachment; liberty therefore means non-impingement by one person on another.

Rousseau put this very clearly when he said: 'The nature of things does not madden us, only ill will does.' Slavery means being a slave to a person, not to the nature of things. Of course, we use the word 'freedom' in various metaphorical senses also. We speak of people not merely as being literally slaves, in the sense in which Uncle Tom was a slave to Simon Legree in the novel *Uncle Tom's Cabin*, but also in the sense in which a man is said to be a slave to his passions, a slave to the bottle, a slave to this, that or the other obsession. This sense of being a slave, though widespread, is nevertheless a metaphor; it is quite clear that there is a more literal and concrete sense in which, if a man is tied to a tree or imprisoned, he cannot by any possible perversion of language be said to be free; whereas a man who simply suffers from other kinds of inability is not usually described as a *slave*. There are all sorts of things I may be unable to do, but this does not make me a slave. I cannot fly to the sky with wings; I cannot count beyond five million; I cannot understand the works of Hegel. There are all sorts of things which I say I cannot do. But because I cannot understand the works of Hegel, and because I cannot fly through the air at more than a certain velocity, I do not describe myself as a slave. To be a slave is not the same thing as to be unable to do something; to be a slave is to be *prevented* from doing something, not by the nature of things, but by other persons. Even economic slavery, which is often referred to in socialist writings, simply means that it is idle to offer rights to people who cannot use them; idle to give the penniless and the starving the right to purchase food and clothes for which they have not got the money. This is usually put by saying that political liberty is useless without economic liberty; but the assumption behind it is that they cannot buy these things, not because of some natural disability, as a cripple cannot walk a long distance because he is a cripple, but because other persons are preventing them. So long as there is not this notion of prevention by persons, the notion of liberty does not arise. Liberty is being free from the intervention, from

the interference, of other persons. When they interfere acciden-
tally, the lack of freedom is due to bad luck or mismanagement;
when they do it deliberately, it is called oppression.

All this may hold for the thinkers of the West, where the
principal problem was to put an end to what were regarded as
the arbitrary rules of certain individuals self-constituted as
authorities over the vast majority. But there is also another
notion of freedom, which blossomed among the Germans, and
to this we must now turn our attention.

The Germans were worried evidently not so much by ill will,
on which Rousseau laid stress, as by the nature of things, which
Rousseau had pronounced irrelevant. To them freedom seemed
to mean freedom from the iron necessities of the universe – not
so much from wicked or foolish persons, or social mismanagement, as from the rigorous laws of the external world.

To some extent this is due to the political state of the Germans
in the eighteenth century. The Germans were, throughout this
period, suffering from the appalling humiliation inflicted upon
them by the victories of Richelieu and Louis XIV of France in
the seventeenth century; and from political divisions, economic
impotence, and the general obscurantism and backwardness of
the average German citizen in the century which followed the
Thirty Years War. Another factor of genuine importance
was the absolute dependence of the German on the arbitrary will
of the Prince, which gave him a sense of being a humbler citizen
of the universe than the triumphant French or the free and
proud English.

To such a man, what does it mean to be free? If you are living
in sad circumstances, the first thing which impinges upon your
consciousness is that there are very few things you *can* do.
Either you have not the material means, or your ruler is unjust,
brutal or stupid. Or there are too many natural misfortunes
which rain down upon you. Or there is some other way in
which you are hemmed in: you are placed in situations where
the number of things which you can do is very small. The
thought of freedom becomes at once something which is in
practice unrealisable and, as an ideal, deeply and passionately
desirable.

The reaction to this situation, which often occurs in the history of humanity, was to say, 'If I cannot get what I want, then perhaps by depriving myself of the want itself I shall make my life happier. Evidently I shall not be made happy by pining to get what powerful persons or adverse circumstances will not let me have. But perhaps by killing within myself the desire for these things I shall achieve that calm and that serenity which is as good a substitute for owning the things which I want as can be found in this vale of tears.'

This was the mood in which, when the Greek city-state was declining, the Stoics and the Epicureans argued. This was the mood in the first century AD in which the Roman Stoics of that period, and indeed the early Christians also, preached their great sermons. This is indeed a truth which became particularly vivid for the Germans of the eighteenth century. There are many things which I want, but circumstances will not let me have them. Well then, I must defend myself against this outer universe, I must somehow contract the area which is vulnerable to these adversities. Instead of trying to lunge forward and obtain things which I cannot get, and merely being defeated and destroyed in the process, I must make a strategic retreat. I must go to a place where the tyrant and evil fortune cannot reach me. If I do not expose so much of myself, so great a surface to these adverse factors, perhaps I shall be safer.

This is psychologically, and indeed sociologically, in part responsible for the doctrine of the unassailable inner life. I try to contract myself into my private world. I say to myself, 'The tyrant wants to deprive me of every opportunity of advancement, the tyrant wants to destroy my substance; very well, let him do so – these things do not matter. What he can have, let him have; I shall cut these things off from myself, for they are of no value to me. If I do not want to keep them, I shall not miss them if they are taken away.' It is a curious, strategic retreat into an inner citadel. I say to myself, 'If I preserve my own spirit, my inward serenity, if I keep myself to my own inner thoughts, if I cultivate inner ideals, the tyrant cannot reach that realm. If my body is exposed to his power, let him have it; if my wealth is something which he can confiscate, let him have it. I shall concentrate upon what is out of his reach – my inner spirit, my inner self.' This is the source of the re-emergence of the doctrine, which has its roots deep both in Christianity and in Judaism, of the two selves: the spiritual, inner, immaterial, eternal soul; and the empirical, outer, physical, material self, which is a prey to every misfortune, which is subject to the iron laws of the material world from which no man may escape.

For natural scientists in the seventeenth and eighteenth centuries, and for some of the *philosophes* of the eighteenth century, too (according to whom man is but a collection of molecules like every other object in nature, and subject to the unalterable laws which govern such molecules), to protest against nature is folly, for we cannot change the material laws of the universe, the physics of it, however oppressive we may find this. And there is no way out.

So there are two enemies from which I must escape. One is the inexorable material laws that govern matter; and the other is the arbitrary will-power of wicked men, the caprice of fortune, and unhappy circumstances. I escape these by what I should like to describe as a very sublime, very grand form of the doctrine of sour grapes. I say that if I cannot have these things, then I do not want them. If I can only kill the desire in myself, the non-satisfaction of it will not irk me. In short, it is a doctrine which says that a desire satisfied and a desire killed come to much the same thing. But this entails various paradoxes. Is a man happier if he has forty desires of which he satisfies only ten, or if he has only two desires and satisfies them both? If freedom means doing what I want, is not a man happier – and freer – who wants less, and therefore has less to do, than a man who wants more and can do far less of what he wants?

It is Rousseau, again, who said that that man is truly free who 'desires what he is able to perform, and does what he desires'. If I desire little, the area within which I can be frustrated is correspondingly smaller. If this view is pushed to the uttermost, it leads almost to suicidal conclusions – literally suicidal ones. I have a pain in my leg. There are two ways of curing it: one is by applying medicine, but the other is by cutting off my leg. The tyrant oppresses me. There are two ways of resisting him: by killing the tyrant, or by making myself impervious to his blows, by not thinking about him, by giving him all he wants, by losing all desire to keep anything of which conceivably, in a moment of the wildest aberration, he might want to rob me. That is essentially the doctrine of the inner self as something not open to any possible attack on or invasion of the outer self – a self about which I no longer care, and which indeed may hurtle on through space governed by the laws of physics and a plaything of wickedness or blind chance.

In Kant's case this led to certain very important consequences which had a profound influence on Fichte and on all the German romantic philosophers and thereby on European consciousness generally. Among these is the doctrine that the only thing which is valuable in the universe is a certain state of this true inner spiritual self. Happiness is something which I may or may not get: it is out of my reach. It depends upon too many material circumstances. To say therefore that the human goal is happiness is to doom man to perpetual frustration and self-destruction. The true ideal cannot rest on something which depends on external circumstances; it must depend upon an inner ideal, and the living up to this inner ideal; upon fulfilling something which my true self commands me to do. The true ideal is to obey the laws of morality. If the laws are issued by some outside force, then I am not free, then I am a slave. But if I order myself to do these things, then, as Rousseau had already said, I am no longer a slave, for I control myself; I am the author of my own conduct, and that is freedom. Kant's profound notion is that what matters, the only thing which is a supreme value for us (and by value one means an end pursued for its own sake, not as a means to something else), the goal which itself justifies everything else and needs no justification in its turn, that for the sake of which we do what we do, and abstain as we abstain, that for the sake of which we act as we act, and, if need be, die – such a sacred, ultimate principle, which governs our conduct, is ordained to us by ourselves. That is why we are free. Therefore, Kant says, the most sacred object in the universe, the only thing which is entirely good, is the good will, that is to say the free, moral, spiritual self within the body.

It is alone sacred, for what else could be sacred, what else could be valuable? I do what I do for the sake of fulfilling the law which I impose upon myself. Utilitarians say that the proper purpose of action is to make as many people happy as possible, and of course, if that is the goal, then it may be possible to sacrifice human beings, even innocent human beings, for the happiness of the rest. Others again say that I must do that which a sacred text, or a religion, or God, has ordained, or do that which the king has ordered me to do, or that which I find myself desiring, or that which my moral system (which I inherit or acquire without questioning it) permits, makes possible.

For Kant this is a kind of blasphemy. For him the only ultimately valuable thing in the universe is the individual human being. To say of a thing that it is valuable is to say that it is an ideal of a human being, something which a human being – as a rational being, he adds – orders himself to do. To what could a human being be sacrificed? Only to something which is superior to, more authoritative, more valuable than, that human being. But nothing can be more valuable than the principle which a human being believes in, for to say of a thing that it is valuable is to say that it is either a means towards, or identical with, something which somebody seeks, for its own sake, wills for its own sake, wills as a rational being.

Kant did talk a great deal about how important it is to emphasise the element of rationality (though what he meant by that has always been very far from clear, at least to some among his students); and he thought that all rational men would therefore necessarily desire the same general kind of conduct. Whether he was right about that or wrong I shall not here ask: that would take us too far afield. What is important to remember in the doctrine is that to say of a thing that it is valuable is to say that it is an ideal for the inner self which must not be impinged upon, must not be ravaged, or enslaved, or exploited, or destroyed, by any outside force. Hence Kant's passionate defence of the individual as the individual. The only thing which is ultimately wrong for him, as it is for Rousseau (though Kant is much more explicit and violent on the subject), is to deprive a human being of the possibility of choice. The only thing which is an ultimate sin is to degrade or humiliate another human being, to treat another human being as if he were not the author of values; for all that is valuable in the universe is what people honour for its own sake. To deceive somebody, to enslave him, to use another human being as a means for my own ends – this is to say that this other human being's ends are not as rational, as sacred as my own; and this is false, because to say of a thing that it is valuable is to say that it is an end, the end of any rational human being. Hence this passionate doctrine, according to which I must respect other human beings, the only entities in the universe to whom I owe absolute respect, because they are the only beings which create values, fulfil values, the only beings whose activities are that for the sake of which everything else is worth doing, for the sake of which life is worth living, or, if need be, sacrificing.

From this it follows further that morality, moral rules, are not something which I can discover as I can discover factual states of affairs. The whole of the eighteenth century – and not merely the eighteenth century, almost the whole history of philosophy, with the exception of the theology of the Jews and the Christians – insists that moral questions can be answered in the way in which other factual questions can be answered. Indeed, I tried to explain earlier how Helvétius and all his friends preached exactly that. For Kant that is not altogether true, and for his successors it becomes less and less true.

To discover what I ought to do I have to hearken to the inner voice. The voice issues commands, injunctions; preaches ideals which I must live up to. To command, to order, to tell me what to do, to issue what Kant called the categorical imperative, is not to say that something *is* the case. It is no use looking in the outside world for moral goals. Moral goals are not things; moral goals are not states of affairs like a growing tree; they are not facts like the fact that Julius Caesar crossed the Rubicon. They are orders or commands, and commands are not true or false, they are not something which can be discovered by observation. Commands may be right or wrong, they may be profound or shallow, they may be wicked or virtuous, they may be intelligible or unintelligible, but they do not *describe* anything. They order, they enjoin and they stimulate.

This is a very important moment in the history of European consciousness. Morality is seen to be not a collection of facts to be discovered by special faculties for discovering moral facts, as many philosophers, from Plato to our own day, have believed to be true; morality is rather something which is ordered, and therefore cannot be discovered. It is invented, not discovered, made, not found. In this respect it becomes akin to artistic creation. Kant, who speaks of objective, universal rules in some sense discovered by the right use of reason, certainly does not draw that quasi-aesthetic conclusion; but he moves us towards it. He believes in universal rational criteria that hold for all men: but his thesis – the language of inner voices – can point elsewhere. By the time we get to the German romantics of the turn of the century, this becomes more explicit. When the artist creates a work of art, what is it that he does? He obeys some kind of inner impulse, he expresses himself. He creates something in answer to some inner demand, he projects himself, he above all does something, acts in a certain way, behaves in a certain fashion, makes something. He does not learn, discover, deduce, calculate, think.

In the case of previous thinkers, you could say that to discover certain things to be true (for example, that happiness is the true goal of man, or that happiness is not a worthy goal for man; that life is material in character or spiritual in character, or whatever it might be) was achieved in a fashion analogous to that in which Newton discovered the physical laws which the universe obeys. But when an artist creates something, is he discovering? Where is the song before it is sung? Where is the song before it is composed? The song is the singing of the song, or the composing of the song. Where is the picture before it is painted? Especially if the picture is non-representative, as music is non-representative, where is the artist's image of his creation before he creates it? The act of the artist is a kind of continuous activity, it is a doing of something, and the justification of it is that it is in obedience to some inner impulse. This obedience to the inner impulse is the realisation of an ideal, that for the sake of which he lives, that to which he dedicates himself and regards as his mission and his calling.

It is important to remember that, although Kant did not draw this conclusion, he did lay the foundation of such a belief with regard to ethics. It has two central elements. The first is that morality is an *activity*. The French Encyclopaedists and the great figures of the German Enlightenment maintained that first we discover the truth in such matters, then we apply our knowledge effectively. But according to this new view morality is not first theory, then practice, but itself a kind of activity. The second element is that this is what is meant by human autonomy. Human autonomy, human independence, means that you are not the prey of some force which you cannot control. I have already quoted Rousseau's dictum that 'The nature of things does not madden us, only ill will does.' But these men fear the force of things even more than the force of persons. Heteronomy, which is the opposite of autonomy, means that I am not independent. I am not independent because I am overcome by passions, because I am overcome by desires or fears or hopes which force me to do various things which I might not, in some deeper sense, wish to do, which I regret afterwards, which I repent of, which I say that, if I were at my best, if I were really I, I would not be doing. Heteronomy means that you are in some way subject to, a slave of, factors over which you have no control. Autonomy is the opposite. Autonomy means that you act as you act because this is your will; *you* are acting – acting, not being acted upon.

This 'you' which is acting is of course not the body, which is prey to every possible physical ill and every possible physical law; it is something else which moves in a free region. Autonomy means the successful self-detachment from any region in which hostile forces or blind forces, or forces for which I am in any case not myself responsible, such as physical laws or the whim of a tyrant, operate. Autonomy, true freedom, consists in issuing orders to myself which I, being free to do as I will, obey. Freedom is obedience to self-imposed injunctions. This is Rousseau's concept of moral freedom, and it is Kant's.

Every human being is such a source of value, and for this reason should be venerated by every other human being. That is why tampering with human beings, 'getting at' them, shaping them, altering them, doing things to them in the name of principles which are objective (that is, outside – valid independently of – human wills), in the way in which Helvétius wanted to do things to them in the name of happiness, is forbidden. That is why all that counts is *motive*. The execution of the plan I am not responsible for, since that is something in which physical laws intervene. I cannot be responsible for doing something of which I am not in control. 'Ought' implies 'can' – if you cannot do something, you cannot be told that you ought to do it. Therefore, if I have duties, if there is a morality, if there are ends, if there are certain things which I ought to do, and others which I ought to avoid, they must be in some region which can be completely free from outside interference. That is why it cannot be my duty to seek happiness, for happiness is out of my control. My duty can be only that which I can wholly control, not the achievement, but the attempt – the setting myself to do what I deem right. I am free only in the fastness of my own inner self.

Certain consequences sprang from this view which had very considerable political effects. The first, immediate effect was a kind of quietism. If all that a man should be promoting is his own inner moral self-protection, if the only thing which counts is the motive, if all that a man can be responsible for is his own personal integrity, that he be honest, that he be truthful, that he at any rate does not cheat, then, whatever may happen to the outside world – the economic and political sphere, the region of material bodies in space liable to be interfered with by outside factors, whether physical or not – all that should be outside the realm of proper moral activity. This is, indeed, how Fichte, in his earlier period, thinks.[1]

Fichte maintained that the individual must be absolutely free.

---

[1] But gradually another thought comes stealing over this original one: that man is not an isolated being, that man is what he is because he is made by society. Here perhaps the German philosopher Herder, about whom I say something later, had a considerable influence on him.

'I am wholly my own creation,' he says; and 'I do not accept the law of what nature offers me because I must, I believe it because I will.'*[1] He says that the important thing is not *das Gegebene* (that which is given) but *das Aufgegebene* (that which is imposed upon me, that which is my duty, that which is ordained, that which is part of my mission). Fichte declares that this law is not itself drawn from the realm of fact, but from our own self, the pure, original form of the self, which is, he says, the creating, the shaping, the forming of things in the outside world according to my ideas and aims, for it is only then that I am their master, that they must serve me.* Hence springs the romantic notion that the most important thing in the world is integrity, dedication.

This is so important an idea that I should like to linger a little on it. In all previous ages of man – since Plato at least – the person who was admired, the person who was looked up to, was the sage. The sage was a man who knew how to live. Some people thought the sage was in contact with God, and that God told him what to do and what the truth was. Some thought the sage was somebody in a laboratory – Paracelsus or Dr Faustus – or again someone who discovered these things by means other than empirical investigation, by some sort of intuitive grasp, by a special insight. Morality was like other forms of knowledge, a process of discovery of certain truths; and the most important thing to aim at was to be in a position to know these truths. If you could not perceive them for yourself, you consulted a specialist; and to be a specialist was admired. The prophet, the seer, the scientist, the philosopher, or whoever it might be, was the person to look up to, because he was the person who knew how to do things, because he knew what the universe was like. The chemist might one day be able to change base metals into gold or discover the elixir of life. The political expert was somebody who knew how to govern because he understood the psychology and physiology of human nature, and of society, and knew enough about the general constitution of the universe to be able to adapt his skill thereto. The person one admired and

---

[1] For the meaning of the asterisks in this chapter see p. 160.

looked up to was the man who got things right, who could discover the correct answer, who knew.

There will be cases where it is necessary not merely to live for the sake of obtaining these goals that you want, in the light of the knowledge which you have, but also to die for them. Christian martyrs died; but what they died for was the truth. They died because they desired, by their example and by their testimony, to witness to those truths, that knowledge, that wisdom which had been vouchsafed to them or to the people in whom they trusted. But the mere act of self-sacrifice, the mere act of dying for your conviction, the mere act of immolating yourself to some inner ideal because it happens to be your ideal and nobody else's – that was not hitherto admired. If a Muslim were brave and died for his faith, you did not spit upon his corpse, you did not mock him. You admired his courage and resolution; you thought it was the greatest of pities that a man so brave, and perhaps naturally so good, should die for so absurd a set of beliefs. But you did not admire him for his dedication to those beliefs.

By the time we get to the early nineteenth century all this has changed. We find that what is admired is *idealism* as such. But what is meant by idealism? An idealist is a person who throws away everything that might attract baser natures – wealth, power, success, popularity – for the sake of serving his inner ideal, for the sake of creating that which his inner self dictates. This is the ideal hero of German romanticism, and of its disciples, Carlyle, Michelet and, in their youth, the Russian radicals. The great artistic figure of the nineteenth century, who impressed himself deeply upon the imagination of Europe, was Beethoven. Beethoven is visualised as a man in a garret, poor, unkempt, neglected, rough, ugly; he has thrown away the world, he will have none of its wealth, and although the rewards are offered, he rejects them. He rejects them in order to fulfil himself, in order to serve the inner vision, in order to express that which demands, with an absolute imperative force, that it be expressed. The worst thing that a man can do is to 'sell out', to betray an ideal. That alone is despicable – despicable because the only thing which makes life worth living (to go back to Kant), the only thing which makes values values, which makes some things right and others wrong, the only thing which can justify conduct, is this inner vision.

The important thing about this attitude, which reaches its height in the early nineteenth century, is that it is no longer relevant, indeed it no longer means much, to ask whether what these people are seeking is true or false.[1] What you admire is a man who hurls himself against the walls of life, who fights against immense odds without asking himself whether the result will be victory or death, and who does this because he cannot act otherwise. The favoured image is that of Luther: there he stands, he cannot move, because he serves his inner ideal. That is what is meant by integrity, devotion, self-fulfilment, self-direction; that is what is meant by being an artist, a hero, a sage and even a good man.

This is quite novel. Mozart and Haydn would have been exceedingly surprised if what was valued in them was an inner spiritual impulse; they were artists who produced musical works which were beautiful, and these works were commissioned by patrons and admired by audiences because they were beautiful. They were craftsmen who made things: they were not priests, they were not prophets, they were purveyors. Some purvey tables, others purvey symphonies; and if the symphonies are good symphonies, still more if they are works of genius, then the persons who write them are, or should be, admired.

By the time we get to the nineteenth century the artist becomes a hero and the act of defiance becomes the central act of his life. You defy the powerful, the rich, the wicked, the philistines, and the dry and critical and mean-spirited intelligentsia if need be – all the people against whom Rousseau hurled his early thunderbolts, followed by Carlyle and Nietzsche and D. H. Lawrence. You defy these people in order to assert yourself, say your word, be something autonomous, not be at the mercy of,

---

[1] Kant spoke about reason and gave certain criteria for determining the difference between false and true moral commandments. But by the time we get to the nineteenth century this is no longer operative.

guided by, conditioned by, things or circumstances other than those which you create out of your own inner self.

So long as it is confined to artists this is a noble ideal which no one today publicly spurns; indeed the moral consciousness of today is largely moulded by these romantic notions, in terms of which we admire idealists and men of integrity, whether we agree with their ideals or not, sometimes even when we think them foolish, in a way in which in the eighteenth century and in previous centuries they were not admired at all, and thought lovable but silly.* But it has a more sinister side to it. Morality now becomes something which is not found but invented; morality is not a set of propositions corresponding to certain facts which we discover in nature. Indeed, nature is nothing to do with it; nature for Kant, nature for Fichte, is simply a collection of dead matter upon which you impose your will. We have departed far indeed from the notion of copying nature, following nature – *naturam sequi* – being like nature. On the contrary, now you mould nature, you transform nature; nature is a challenge, nature is simply the raw material. If this is so, if morality consists in projecting yourself in some way, it may be that political activity is also a kind of self-projection. Napoleon, who projects his personality across the map of Europe, who moulds human beings in France, in Germany, in Italy, in Russia, as the artist moulds his material, as the composer moulds sound and the painter colours – Napoleon is the highest expression of morality,[1] for he is expressing his personality, he is asserting himself, he is serving the inner ideal which drives him on and on.

At this point there is a quantum leap in Fichte's thought – from the isolated individual to the group as a true subject or self. How does this arise?

I am only free if I do things which nobody can stop me from doing, and I only do this if it is my inner self which is active, not impinged upon by anything else.* A self is a spirit, but it is not an isolated spirit, and it is here that Fichte begins on that path which leads to such peculiar conclusions, that path which begins

---

[1] Though not, as it happens, for Fichte, who had a particular hatred for Napoleon as a false artist, alien to spiritual values.

to move towards the notion that selves are not individual human beings at all, that the self is something to do with society, that perhaps the self, the human self, is really not only itself the product of history and of tradition, but also bound to other human beings by Burke's myriad indissoluble spiritual links, that it exists only as part of a general pattern, of which it forms an element. So much so that it becomes misleading to say that a self is an empirical individual born in a certain year, living a certain kind of life, in a certain physical environment, and dying in a certain place at a certain date. Fichte begins to move towards a theological conception of the self; he says that the true, free self is not the empirical self which is clothed in a body and has a date and a place,* it is a self which is common to all bodies, it is a super-self, it is a larger, divine self which he gradually begins to identify, now with nature, now with God, now with history, now with a nation.[1]

Starting with the notion of the isolated individual who serves some inner ideal which is out of reach of nature or the tyrant, Fichte gradually adopts the idea that the individual himself is nothing, that man is nothing without society, that man is nothing without the group, that the human being hardly exists at all. The individual, he begins to suspect, does not exist, he must vanish. The group – *Gattung* – alone exists, is alone real.

It begins innocently enough. The individual man must endeavour to repay his debt to society. He must take his place among men, he must strive in some respect to advance the rest of humanity, which has done so much for him. 'Man', he says, 'only becomes man among other men.' And again: 'Man is destined to live in society; he must do so; he is not a complete

---

[1] There is a peculiar, special process of metaphysical insight which only a few chosen men in each generation – in particular Fichte himself – can use for the purpose of discovering what is the duty of man, given to this special active insight, the free self within me, the self which a tyrant cannot reach, which alone is free. To go through this process is for Fichte analogous to the procedure of the ancient mystics, the ancient seers and prophets who felt themselves in the presence of something greater than themselves, greater than their physical selves, greater than their empirical selves – in the presence of some vast power: God, nature, the real self.

human being, he contradicts his own nature, if he lives in isolation.'*

Fichte gradually came to believe something of this kind. But he goes much further. The real self of Fichte's fully developed philosophy is not you, nor I, nor any particular individual, nor any particular group of individuals. It is that which is common to all men; it is a personified, embodied principle which, like a pantheistic divinity, expresses itself through finite centres, through me, through you, through other people. Its embodiment on earth is the true society, conceived as a collection of persons bound together metaphysically, like small flames issuing from some great central fire. It is the great central fire towards which each flame tends in the process of being aware of the moral orders – which are impulsions, flame-like strivings – of its inner self.* This is a theological doctrine, and Fichte clearly was in this sense a theologian, and so was Hegel, and no good purpose is served by supposing that they were secular thinkers. They were deeply influenced by the Christian tradition, and it might seem to some that they were heretics in it. But theologians they were, far more theological than what is called philosophical at the present time.

In this way Fichte gradually moves from the group to the notion that the true person, the true individual, whose act of self-assertion is the march of morality in history – the imposition of moral imperatives upon a pliant, flexible nature – this individual is not even the human being at his most self-conscious, but a collectivity: race, nation, mankind.* This was the substance of those celebrated speeches of his to the German nation delivered in Berlin in 1807–8, at a time when the troops of Napoleon were occupying the city, in which he told the Germans to arise and resist. Let me quote from these to show the kind of thing he had in mind, and how far he must have travelled. Fichte is speaking of the German character, and he says that there are two kinds of characters in the world:

Either you believe in an original principle in man – in a freedom, a perfectibility and infinite progress of our species – or you believe in none of this. You may even have a feeling or intuition of the

68

opposite. All those who have within them a creative quickening of life, or else, assuming that such a gift has been withheld from them, at least reject what is but vanity and await the moment when they are caught up by the torrent of original life, or even if they are not yet at this point, at any rate have some confused presentiment of freedom, those who have towards it not hatred, nor fear, but a feeling of love – all these are part of the primal humanity, and considered as a people they constitute the primal people. In short, the people. I mean the German people. All those, on the other hand, who have resigned themselves to represent only derivative, second-hand products, who think of themselves in this way, these become in effect such and shall pay the price of their belief. They are only an annexe to life. Not for them those pure springs which flowed before them, which still flow around them; they are but the echo coming back from a rock of a voice which is silent. Considered as a people, they are excluded from the primal people, they are strangers, outsiders. A nation which to this day bears the name of German (or simply the people) has not ceased to give evidence of a creative and original activity in most diverse fields. The hour has come at last when philosophy, penetrated through and through by self-awareness, will hold to this nation a mirror wherein it will recognise itself with a clear perception, and at the same time will become quite clearly aware of the mission of which it has hitherto had but a confused premonition, but which nature herself has imposed upon that nation; an unmistakable call has been addressed to it today to labour in freedom calmly and clearly and to perfect itself according to the notions which it has framed of itself, to accomplish the duty which has been outlined to it.

And everyone who believes this kind of thing will join with these people whose function, whose mission, is to create. All those who believe on the contrary in an arrested being, or in retrogression or in cycles of history; or else those who put an inanimate nature at the helm of the world, whatever be their native country, whatever be their language, they are not Germans, they are strangers to us and one should hope they will be utterly cut off from our people.

Then the great paean begins, the great nationalist chauvinist cry. Individual self-determination now becomes collective self-realisation, and the nation a community of unified wills in pursuit of moral truth. But this collective march forward would be directionless if the nation were not led, if it were not illuminated by the quasi-divine leadership of the *Zwingherr*. Fichte says, 'What we need is a leader; what we need is a man to mould us.' 'Hither!' he suddenly cries '*Zwingherr zur Deutschheit* [the man who will compel us to Germanism]. We hope, of course, that it will be our King who will perform this service, but be he who he may we must await him till he comes and moulds us, till he comes and makes us.'

In short, we have come full circle. We started with the notion of an autonomous person, anxious not to be impinged upon, wishing for a life of absolute freedom, obeying only the inner workings of its own inner consciousness, of its own inner conscience. And now we say: Life is art, life is a moulding, life is the creation of something – self-creation – by a so-called 'organic' process.* There are superior beings and there are inferior beings, as there is within me a higher and a lower nature, and I can rise to great heights in a moment of crisis, and crush my passions and desires and perform heroic acts of self-immolation in the name of a principle which raises me; which, as he says, catches me up in a flow of life. If I can suppress that which is lower in me, then the leader or the race can suppress that which is lower in it, as the spirit does the sinning flesh.

Here it is at last, the famous and fatal analogy between the individual and the nation, the organic metaphor which leaves the field of theological imagery and is secularised by Burke and by Rousseau, and is very powerful in Fichte. Fichte contrasts *compositum*, which is a mere artificial combination, and *totum*, which is a total nation, which is something organic, single, whole, and in which the higher principle dominates, the higher principle which may take the shape of a great nation, or of history.* And the greatest agent of this force is a divine conqueror or leader whose business it is to play upon his nation as an artist plays upon his instrument, to mould it into a single organic whole, as the painter, the sculptor moulds his materials, as the composer creates patterns of sound.

As for freedom, individual freedom and individual conscience, and right and wrong, whether discovered or invented, what has become of those now? What of that individual freedom of which we spoke earlier, which the British and the French writers defended, the freedom of each man to be allowed, within certain limits at least, to live as he likes, to waste his time as he likes, to go to the bad in his own way, to do that which he wants simply because freedom as such is a sacred value? Individual freedom, which in Kant has a sacred value, has for Fichte become a choice made by something super-personal. It chooses me, I do not choose it, and acquiescence is a privilege, a duty, a self-lifting, a kind of self-transcendent rising to a higher level. Freedom, and morality generally, is self-submission to the super-self – the dynamic cosmos. We are back with the view that freedom *is* submission.

Fichte himself largely thought in terms of some transcendental, idealistic will-power which had relatively little to do with the actual terrestrial life of men, and only towards the end of his life did he perceive the possibility of moulding earthly life in conformity with these transcendental desires. But his followers translated it into more mundane terms. The transfer of emphasis from reason to will created that notion of freedom which is not the notion of non-interference, not the notion of permitting each man to have his choice, but the notion of self-expression, the notion of imposing yourself upon the medium, the notion of freedom as the removal of obstacles to yourself. One can only remove obstacles by subjugating them: in mathematics, by understanding; in material life, by acquisition; in politics, by conquest. That is at the heart of the notion that a free nation is a victorious nation, that freedom is power and that conquest and freedom are one.

To show what this has led to, let me quote a very shrewd observer, the German poet Heinrich Heine, then living in Paris. These were the lines which he wrote in 1834 in an attempt to warn the French not to minimise the force of ideas:

The idea tries to become action, the word desires to be made flesh, and lo, a man . . . has only to express his thought, and the world forms itself . . . The world is but the outer manifestation of the word.

Note this, you proud men of action, you are nothing but the

unconscious tools of the men of thought, who in humble stillness have often drawn up your most definite plans of action. Maximilien Robespierre was nothing but the hand of Jean-Jacques Rousseau, the bloodstained hand that drew from the womb of time the body whose soul Rousseau had created ... the *Critique of Pure Reason* by Kant ... is the sword with which deism was beheaded ...

Fichte was once well paraphrased by the American philosopher Josiah Royce thus: 'The world is the poem ... dreamed out by the inner life.' So, then, our worlds are literally different if we differ spiritually. A composer, a banker, a robber literally create their worlds. Whether or not he was thinking of this, Heine feels genuine terror before this attitude, and had a genuine vision of doom to come: 'Kantians will appear, who in the world of mere phenomena hold nothing sacred, and ruthlessly with sword and axe will hack through the foundations of our European life, and pull up the past by its last remaining roots. Armed Fichteans will come, whose fanatical wills neither fear nor self-interest can touch.' These men, these pantheists, will fight recklessly for their principles, for these principles are absolute, and their dangers seem to them purely illusory. *Naturphilosophen* will identify themselves with elemental forces, which are always destructive. Then the god Thor will wield his gigantic hammer and smash the Gothic cathedrals. Christianity was the only force which held back the ancient German barbarians with its naked violence; once that talisman is broken a terrible cataclysm will break out. 'Don't try [he says to the French] to suppress or to extinguish the flame, you will only burn your fingers.' Above all, don't laugh at the dreamy poet and his revolutionary fancies.

Thought precedes action as lightning precedes thunder. German thunder too is a German, and not in a hurry, and it comes rolling slowly onward; but come it will, and once you hear it crashing, as nothing ever crashed before in the history of the world, then know that the German thunder has finally hit the mark. At that sound the eagles will fall dead from the air and the lions in the remotest deserts of Africa will ... creep to their royal lairs. A drama will be performed in Germany in contrast with which the French Revolution will seem a mere peaceful idyll.

The French are warned not to clap this great gladiatorial show which will begin in Germany. 'For you', he says to them, 'liberated Germany is more dangerous than the whole Holy Alliance, with all its Cossacks and its Croats. For ... we Germans forget nothing', and pretexts for war will be found. The French are warned, above all, not to disarm. Remember, he says to them, that upon Olympus, 'amidst the nude deities who feast upon nectar and ambrosia, there is one goddess who amidst all this merriment and peace keeps her armour and her helmet and a spear in her hand – the goddess of wisdom'.

This prophecy was destined to be fulfilled. It is idle to blame any one thinker, any one philosopher, for the actions of multitudes in history. Nevertheless it is odd to reflect that there is a direct line, and a very curious one, between the extreme liberalism of Kant, with his respect for human nature and its sacred rights, and Fichte's identification of freedom with self-assertion, with the imposition of your will upon others, with the removal of obstacles to your desires, and finally with a victorious nation marching to fulfil its destiny in answer to the internal demands given to it by transcendental reason, before which all material things must crumble. We have indeed travelled a long way from the Anglo-French notion of freedom which allowed each man his own circle, that small but indispensable vacuum within which he can do as he pleases, go to the bad or go to the good, choose for the sake of choosing, in which the value of choice as such is regarded as sacred.

These are the two notions of liberty which were spread over Europe at the beginning of the nineteenth century; to ask which of them is true, and which of them is false, is a shallow and unanswerable question. They represent two views of life of an irreconcilable kind, the liberal and authoritarian, open and closed, and the fact that the word 'freedom' has been a genuinely central symbol in both is at once remarkable and sinister.

HEGEL

OF ALL THE IDEAS that originated during the period which I am discussing, the Hegelian system has perhaps had the greatest influence on contemporary thought. It is a vast mythology which, like many other mythologies, has great powers of illumination as well as great powers of obscuring whatever it touches. It has poured forth both light and darkness – more darkness perhaps than light, but about that there will be no agreement. At any rate, it is like a very dark wood, and those who once enter it very seldom come back to tell us what it is that they have seen. Or, when they do, like those who are addicted to the music of Wagner, their ear appears permanently attuned to sounds very unlike the older, simpler and nobler harmonies which once they used to listen to. As a result it is not always very easy to understand, through the new terminology which the system seems to induce in them, what their vision really consists of.

One thing is certain. Followers of Hegel claim that, whereas previously they saw things only from the outside, they now see them from the inside. Whereas previously they saw merely the outer surface, the shell, they now see the inner essence, the inner purpose; the essential end towards which things tend. They have an 'inside' as opposed to an 'outside' view, and this difference between outside and inside is crucial to the understanding of the whole system.

When we look at material objects – tables, chairs, trees, stones – all that we see is a variety of objects, and movements among these objects, and we can describe them and classify them, and concentrate our classifications into general formulae which enable us to describe and predict their behaviour, and perhaps say something about their past also. When one asks why things happen as they do, there are two senses of this word 'why'. In one sense natural science does answer the question. If I say, 'Why does the table not fly upwards, but on the whole stay on the ground?', a great many physical facts will be offered me about molecules and their relations, and I shall be told about the physical laws which operate on these molecules. All this does, however, is to give me very general laws about the characteristics of objects which resemble each other. Newton and Galileo showed themselves to be men of genius in reducing to a minimum the number of formulae in terms of which I can classify the behaviour of objects, so that I can do so as economically and manageably as possible.

But suppose I ask a very different sort of question. Suppose I say, 'I perfectly understand what you are telling me; you are describing what this table does; all you are telling me is that the table does not, for example, fly upwards, but stays on the ground, because it belongs to a class of entities which are in general subject to the laws of gravitation. But I want to know something rather different: I want to know why it does it, in the sense in which I ask what the meaning of its behaviour is, or rather what the purpose is of what it does. Why was the world arranged in such a way that tables do not, in fact, fly upwards? Why do trees, for example, grow while tables do not?' This 'Why?' is not answered by reciting what happens, nor even by providing very powerful laws in terms of which I can determine the position and movement of every molecule. I want to know why things happen in the sense of the word 'why' in which I ask the question, 'Why did such and such a man strike such and such another man?' In that case you would not simply answer, 'Because certain molecules rotating in a certain manner produced a certain effect in his bloodstream which gradually affected his muscles in such a way that his arm rose', and so forth. In a sense all this is true, and you could say it, and yet it would not be an answer to the question which I am asking. You would be answering my question much more naturally if you said that he did it because he was angry, or in order to accomplish this or that end. He did it in order to avenge himself; he did it in order to obtain the satisfaction of giving pain to the person whom he struck. It seems quite clear that, whereas we can ask that kind of question about persons, perhaps a little less certainly about animals, much less certainly about, say, trees, it is not sensible to ask such questions about material objects, or about a great many entities in the universe which do not appear to be animate.

According to the great German romantic philosophers, the crime of eighteenth-century science, and to some extent of seventeenth-century science too, or anyway of their philosophical interpreters, was to amalgamate these two kinds of explanation; to say that there was only one kind of explanation, namely the kind which applies to material objects; to say that, in asking the question 'Why?', we only mean to ask for facts. We are asking 'What happens? When does it happen? Next door to what does it happen? What happens after what, and before what?' and never 'What purposes does it pursue? What goals? Why does it do it?' in the sense in which I can ask 'Why does a person do something?' That is why Descartes said that history was not a science – because there were no general laws which could be applied to history. The whole thing was much too fluid, the number of differences was far greater than the number of similarities, it was impossible to collect so unstable a subject-matter, about which so little was known, where there were so few repetitions, so few uniformities, into any form which could be subsumed under a few powerful formulae. Therefore he regarded history as simply a collection, ultimately, of gossip, travellers' tales, something scarcely worthy of the name of science. Indeed, the general ideal of the seventeenth-century scientists was not to concern oneself over-much with anything which could not be dealt with by lucid and systematic methods; and systematic methods meant the methods of natural science.

One of the great advances made in the late eighteenth century and the early nineteenth was to revise this conception. Perhaps this was not the last word which could be said; perhaps the question 'Why?' was more interesting than it had been made out to be. When, for example, Vico – an Italian thinker of the early eighteenth century who was unjustly neglected although he was a bold and original genius – began to write about history, he said that to treat human beings as objects, like tables and chairs and trees, was absurd; that we knew more about human beings, in a certain sense, than we knew about natural objects; and that the whole of the prestige of the natural sciences was founded on a mistake. In the case of tables and stones we could only say what they looked like to us, and also what at any given moment they consisted of, what there was before them and what there was after them, what there was next door to them – we could simply place them in a sort of inventory of the universe in time and space and number. But we could do more than this in the case of history. If we are asked why Julius Caesar acted as he did, we do not just give a physical description of his body and movements. We tend to talk about his motives. We cannot talk about the motives of tables and chairs, even assuming that we think they might have such motives, because we do not know what it is like to be a table or to be a chair, only what they look like. But according to Vico we know more than this about Caesar, by a species of imaginative insight. By analogy with ourselves we know that he possessed a will, emotions, feelings, that he was, in short, a human being. We can try to talk about historical personages as we would talk about ourselves, and explain not merely what they did, but also what their purposes were, what their ends were, what their 'inner feelings' were. It is this distinction between inner and outer which becomes of importance.

Similarly, the German eighteenth-century metaphysician Herder thought that if we try to describe the life of a nation, it is natural to ask 'What is it like to belong to such and such a nation?' Then it is natural to ask 'What does it mean to "belong" at all?' If I say 'So and so is a German', it is not enough merely to say that he was born in a certain country, in a certain climate, on a certain date, and that he has certain physiological or physical resemblances to certain other persons also called Germans. When I say that he 'belongs' to them, and still more when I say that he 'feels that he belongs' to them, that he 'feels himself to be a German', this means at least that he likes what other

Germans like, likes German songs, likes the way in which Germans eat and drink, likes the way in which they live, the way in which they make their laws and the way in which they tie their shoes. To feel oneself a German is to have a certain connection with other Germans which cannot be exhausted by a mere material or physical description of outer behaviour, as a behaviourist would record it. When I say of someone that he is a German, and that he thrills to the sound of German songs, or that his heart rises when he sees a German flag fly, the very words 'German songs' are not to be analysed in a purely materialistic or scientific, physical fashion. To be a German song is to be produced in a certain way by certain people with certain purposes; and the song itself must, I will not say 'possess a certain flavour', but it must possess a certain kind of expressiveness; it must spring from or express a certain kind of character, outlook, attitude to life. This attitude to life, this specific character which a song expresses, will also be expressed by much larger and more permanent institutions – by the German system of legislation, by their political system, by the way in which they treat each other, by their accent, by the shape of their handwriting, and by everything which they do and are and feel.

What is this common quality which makes a people German? According to Herder it is belonging to a certain individual group. What is meant by individual? Herder's point was that when you talk about purposes you need not and should not confine yourself to individuals. When you ask why so and so does this or that, you normally answer in psychological terms – 'Because he wants to', 'Because he proposes to.' But you can also ask about impersonal entities. You can say 'Why do the Germans write in Gothic script, whereas the French do not?' This kind of 'Why?' will be answered in a manner much more like the way in which I answer questions such as 'Why does so and so eat with a spoon, whereas somebody else eats with his fingers?' than like the way in which I respond when asked 'Why do these molecules have this effect, whereas other molecules have quite a different one?'

This means that we are trembling on the verge of the notion of impersonal or super-personal or collective purposes. This, of course, is the beginning of a mythology, but a very convenient mythology, for otherwise we certainly do not know how to speak about groups and societies. When we say that a nation has a peculiar genius – that the Portuguese genius is quite different from the Chinese genius – we are not saying that a given average Portuguese is a man of genius and different from a given Chinese man of genius. We are trying to say that the way in which the Portuguese build their ships, the way in which they express their views, have something in common, a kind of family resemblance or family face which pervades everything, and that it is quite different from the corresponding resemblance among the Chinese; and this indication of the family face, the analysis of what it consists in, we call historical explanation. When someone says 'Why does so and so write as he does?' we do take it for an answer if you reply that it is because he belongs to the Portuguese family of nations, because he belongs to a particular group of persons who live in Brazil or Portugal or Goa and who have a certain outlook, certain kinds of values, who feel familiar with certain kinds of experience but feel that certain other kinds of experience are wholly alien to them. This is an answer to the question 'Why?' which is quite different from the answer given by the sciences, and this is the kind of 'Why?' which Vico and Herder dealt with. It is this which Hegel tried to generalise, his view being that all questions about the universe could be answered in this 'deeper' sense of 'Why?'

He formulated this by saying that the universe was really the self-development of the world spirit. A world spirit is something like an individual spirit, except that it embraces and is identical with the whole universe. If you can imagine the universe as a kind of animate entity possessing a soul in roughly the same sense as, but no doubt grander than, that in which individuals possess souls, intentions, purposes, wills, then you can ask 'Why do things happen as they do?' They happen as they do because they are part of a vast spiritual movement which has purposes, intentions and a direction, very much as human beings have purposes, intentions and a direction. How do we know what that direction is? Because we are parts of it. Because every individual is a finite element in an infinite whole which, collectively speaking, possesses a certain purpose and a certain direction.

But, you may say, what is the evidence for this? Certainly Hegel does not provide anything which can be called empirical or scientific evidence. Ultimately it turns out to be a case of metaphysical insight or an act of faith. If what he says were not so, he claims, then there would be too many 'brute' facts. You would be asking why stones are as they are, why plants are as they are, and the answer would be, 'In your sense of the word "why", namely, if you are asking who intended them for what, we cannot answer the question.' Vico had already said that only those who make things can truly understand their nature. The novelist understands everything there is to be understood about his characters because he creates them; there is nothing there which he does not know, because he has made them. In this sense of understanding, only God can understand the universe, for he has made it, and we can understand only those finite things which we make. A watchmaker understands a watch as a novelist understands his characters.

But now you may ask, 'What about other human beings? Can we not understand them?' There is obviously a sense in which, when they talk to us or when they show certain moods, when they look gloomy or dejected or happy or gay or fierce, we are able to understand what they are at, in a different sense from that in which we understand stones and tables. We do not enquire about the outlooks or purposes of tables. In short, we do not think that tables are 'at' anything; they are what they are. The question 'What is a table at?' seems absurd because it appears to make the table an animated entity; it appears to make it sentient, when in fact we suspect that it is not. But we *can* ask this about other human beings, and Hegel – and the romantics generally – suppose that this is because in some sense we participate in this one general 'spirit' of which all human beings are finite centres, and we have a species of metaphysical grasp of – quasi-telepathic insight into – what people are like, because we are human beings ourselves. Therefore history is solely an account of the experiences of human beings. Tables and chairs have no history because they have no experience. History is the story of human creation, human imagination, human wills and intentions, feelings, purposes, everything which human beings do and feel, rather than what is done to them. Human history is something which we create by feeling, by thinking, by being active in some fashion, and therefore, by creating it, we are able to understand it, which is why the understanding of history is an 'inside' view, whereas our understanding of tables and chairs is an 'outside' view.[1]

This being so, Hegel is able to say that, since the whole universe is an enormous sentient whole, we are able to understand what each part of it is doing, provided that we have a sufficiently clear degree of metaphysical insight, such as is possessed, for instance, by the most powerful minds, the most penetrating intelligences. If it were not so, then there would be 'mere' facts which could not be explained at all. If I asked 'Why is this stone lying on the ground, whereas that stone is falling through the air?' I should have to reply that that sort of 'Why?' is not asked in the case of stones; it just is so, it is a brute fact. But for Hegel and for all the metaphysicians of his way of thinking the brute fact is an offence to reason. We cannot 'accept' brute facts because they are not to be explained, and just lie there as a challenge to our understanding. Unless we can relate them to a purposive system, unless they can be fitted into a pattern, they remain unexplained. But what is a pattern? A pattern is something which a plan has. The painting has a pattern because somebody planned it that way. The symphony has a pattern because that alone is what causes its various parts to 'make sense'; because there is a total purpose which the symphony subserves, whether in the mind of the composer who composed it, whether on the part of the musicians who play it, or on the part of the audience which listens to it, a purpose in terms of which the various elements of the symphony, namely the various sounds, function together in a pattern. Unless we can grasp the pattern, we do not 'understand'.

This is the special kind of understanding which means

---

[1] With the justice of this distinction I do not here wish to deal: it would take us too far afield.

perception of patterns. This is the sense in which we understand what it is to be a German, what it is to be a Frenchman. To be a German is to be part of a general German pattern, a pattern which includes undergoing German experiences, German hopes and fears, the way in which a German walks, the way in which he gets up, the way in which he holds his head – everything about him. If we then ask 'Well, what part does he play in the larger pattern of which the entire universe consists?' the answer is that this can only be discovered by somebody who sees the whole. But only the whole, if it were conscious of itself, would see itself as a whole. We are confined to seeing parts. Some see greater parts, some smaller ones, but it is in perceiving things as parts of larger things that any degree of understanding is achieved.

Here arises the further question, 'How in fact does the spirit work? What is the mechanism, what is the pattern?' Hegel thought he had found the answer to that. He said that it worked according to what he called the dialectic. The dialectic for him really makes sense only in terms of thought or artistic creation; and he applies it to the universe because he thinks that in the universe is a kind of act of thought, or a kind of act of self-creation; *self*-creation, for there exists nothing else.[1] In what way does the dialectic work? It works in a way rather like that in which people work when they try to think of answers to questions. First, an idea occurs in my mind, then this idea is qualified by other ideas and does not stay. Other ideas come into collision with it and then, out of the collision and conflict of an idea and the qualifications – the idea and the criticism of the idea, the idea and other ideas which come falling upon it, impinging upon it – something else is born which is neither the first idea, nor the idea which is in opposition to the first idea; rather it is something which retains elements of both but, as he says, rises above them, or transcends them – a synthesis. The first idea is called *thesis*, the second *antithesis*, the third *synthesis*.

---

[1] For him there is no personal deity. If he was a Christian, he was a very heretical one, because he believed in the identity of the creative principle, that is God, with the whole of the universe.

So for example (though Hegel does not use this particular metaphor) in a symphonic work you have a theme consisting of a phrase of music or a melody, then you have a melody which as it were runs against it, and something happens which cannot be called the cancellation of the first theme by the second nor the continuation of the first into the second, but is rather some kind of fusion which destroys the first two ideas and produces something which is half familiar because it grows in some way out of the collision and conflict of the first two and yet is something new. This, according to Hegel, is how the universe works. It works like this because that is how patterns work in thought and in every kind of conscious activity of which we know anything – and he distinguishes the universe into conscious and self-conscious and unconscious ingredients.

Plants and animals are conscious; that is to say they have purposes of some kind, they have low-grade volitions – low-grade thoughts perhaps. Human beings alone are self-conscious, because they not only have thoughts but can watch this dialectical process in themselves. They can see this development, this collision of ideas, the irregular line which their lives follow; how they first do one thing, then half not-do it, and then the doing and the not-doing fuse themselves into a new kind of doing. They can follow this twisting, spiral process in themselves. He tries to explain whole civilisations in these terms. His point is that in the eighteenth century people were able to explain differences but not change. For example, Montesquieu was very convincing and subtle in explaining how climate affected people, Helvétius may have been very penetrating in explaining how education or environment affected them; other eighteenth-century thinkers, by making over-close analogies between human beings and insentient entities, explained how human beings came to be what they were, to some degree, certainly how their bodies came to be what they were, perhaps their nervous systems, perhaps other aspects of them. But how are we to account for change? After all, Italy in Roman days and Italy now are physically much the same country. The seas which wash it affect it in the same way, its climate has not altered abruptly, nor its vegetation. Yet modern Italians are utterly different from ancient Romans.

The characteristic thinkers of the eighteenth century maintained that this was due to human development. It was the result of education and government; and it was because (people like Helvétius thought) human beings were governed, or rather misgoverned – a great many knaves, or perhaps a great many fools, misgoverned a great many fools – that the disasters occurred of which all history up to the beginning of the rational period of human existence was so full. This, for Hegel, is plainly not good enough. If human beings are as much under the influence of external causes as eighteenth-century science, needing to be materialistic, must maintain, then the vast differences, the growth and the development, cannot be explained. This can only be explained by the dialectic, namely by some process of movement, by a dynamism of some sort. This collision of thesis and antithesis, this perpetual clash of forces, is what is responsible for progress. These forces are not merely thoughts in people's heads; they 'incarnate themselves' in institutions, in Churches, in political constitutions, perhaps in vast human enterprises, in migrations of peoples, in revolutions, for example, or in vast intellectual developments, where the thesis and antithesis in their state of continual mutual inner tension grow to a climax. There is an outburst, and the synthesis comes to be born, like a kind of phoenix, from the ashes of the thesis and antithesis.

This need not take concrete physical forms. It need not take the form of a bloodstained revolution. It may only take the form of a vast cultural awakening, like the Renaissance, or some enormous artistic or intellectual or spiritual discovery. But always it takes the form of a leap forward. The process is not continuous, it moves in jumps. First the growing tension of the force and its opposite, then the climax and the enormous jump, the vast spring which the human mind – not necessarily only the human mind, but the whole of the universe – takes on to some new level, on to a new shelf. Then once more the process begins; the new creation is eaten out by its own inner opposing forces until the tension again grows to a climax and the next leap occurs. For Hegel, that is history, that is what explains the discontinuities and tragedies. The tragedies of life consist in this inevitable conflict, but unless there were these conflicts, between nation and nation, between institution and institution, between one form of art and another, between one cultural movement and another, there would be no movement; unless there was friction, there would be death. That is why there is something shallow, for him, something inadequate in the eighteenth-century explanation of evil, sorrow, suffering and tragedy as simply due to mistakes, bad arrangements, inefficiency, so that in the efficient universe all this would be smoothed out, and there would be complete harmony. But for Hegel conflict is the very symptom of development, growth, something occurring, the stream of life beating against the shell of some earlier experience, from which it will presently burst, thus relegating the shell to the slag-heap of those bits of experience, those bits of history, which are done with and are now consigned to some dead past.

Sometimes this development occurs in the form of national activities; sometimes there are individual heroes who personify these leaps – Alexander, Caesar, Napoleon. Certainly these individuals destroyed much; certainly they caused a great deal of suffering. That is the inevitable consequence of any kind of advance. Unless there is friction, there is no progress. Before Hegel, Kant, and before him Mandeville, and to some extent Vico, had already said something of this kind.

Now the question arises: 'What is meant by saying that history is a rational process?' For Hegel, to say that a process is rational is to say that when you grasp what it is, in the only way you can ever really understand anything, that is, by means of a faculty he calls reason, then you see that the process is inevitable. It cannot happen otherwise than as it does. Hegel's train of thought goes somewhat as follows. How do we ever learn a truth, say that twice two equals four? At first it faces us like a brute fact. The schoolboy has to learn the multiplication table by heart in the beginning; he does not understand why two times two must equal four. Hence it is a burden upon his intellect and memory, a dogma which it is his task to learn and remember. Only when he has learned the axioms and the rules of arithmetic does he realise that two times two not merely *is* four, but cannot be other than four. He need not repeat it by rote: it has become part of his natural skill in adding or multiplying. So, when we study history, Hegel supposes, we reach a sufficiently rational level, we rise to a certain stage of illumination in which we begin to understand that historical events not merely happened as they did, but *had* to happen as they did, necessarily; not in the sense of the mechanical causality with which physics deals but rather, for example, in the sense in which we follow the stages of a mathematical argument, where there are rigorous rules; or perhaps even of a symphony, where there are not quite such fixed rules, but we can say that each successive portion is, as it were, inevitable, or, as Hegel might say, a 'rational successor' of the previous portion, so that we say the earlier stage 'does not make sense' unless the later stage is there to complete it, in the way in which the pattern of the carpet can be traced. When we have learned arithmetic and music in this way, we move freely in the mathematical or musical world. The pattern becomes identified with our own mode of thought and feeling and action. We no longer feel it to be external or oppressive to us, or that there are grim *de facto* laws hemming us in to which we must adjust ourselves, but which are not part of what we are, what we want – of our own lives.

According to Hegel, the usual way in which one approaches the external world is by distinguishing between what you want – your intentions, your policies, what you are after – and, on the other hand, what is outside: the things and persons who, just by being there, obstruct the full, free development of your personality. But when you discover why everything is as it is – *must* be so – in the very act of understanding this you will lose the desire for it to be otherwise. When you learn not merely that two times two equals four, but also why, you can no longer wish it to be otherwise. You do not want twice two to be five. Twice two not merely *is* four, but you want it to be so; it is part of the rational

pattern of your thought. The rules of arithmetic become assimilated into the general rules of reasoning, into the way in which
you think and act.

This notion of assimilation is vital in Hegel, because he thinks
of laws not in the way in which science and even common sense
tend to think of them, namely as generalisations of what
happens, but rather more as rules, patterns, forms, in the sense in
which arithmetic proceeds by rules – or logic, or architecture, or
music. To think of a general law as something which you do not
want to be otherwise than as it is, is to think of it as a rule with
which you identify yourself, the method in terms of which you
naturally think, or which you naturally apply, and not as an iron
law discovered to operate outside you, an unbreakable inescapable barrier against which you beat in vain. But rules and
methods presuppose users of them – persons. You employ rules,
or apply them, or live by them; and if the universe obeys rules, it
is not far from this to the idea of it as a vast drama in which the
characters fulfil parts assigned to them. But then there must be a
dramatist; and if you can now imagine the characters in the
confidence of the dramatist, understanding his intentions, you
will arrive at something like the Hegelian notion of how the
world functions.

It is an old theological or metaphysical belief that laws, which
at first seem barriers, something you cannot overcome, gradually
work themselves into your very self, once you understand their
purposes, and you begin using them easily and freely yourself.
Thus, when you become a mathematician, you think in mathematical terms almost unconsciously; and likewise you write
correctly after you have assimilated the rules of grammar,
without feeling that a terrible external strait-jacket of despotic
rules and regulations has been imposed upon you. If you can get
on such terms with nature, consciously identify with her
workings so closely that her laws coincide with the rules and
patterns of your own reasonings and volitions and feelings, then
you obtain the inside view. You are then said to be 'at one' with
nature in her purposes, her intentions. This union, this being at
one with the universe, has always been, in one way or another,
the goal of all the great mystics and metaphysicians. Hegel

expounds this notion in ponderous, obscure and occasionally majestic language. From it he derives his notorious paradox that liberty is the recognition of necessity.

One of the oldest problems of politics, as it is in life, in metaphysics and morals and everything else, is this: if I am completely determined, if some omniscient observer can foresee every single move which I make, how can I possibly be said to be free? If everything I have done in the past, am doing in the present and will do in the future can be accounted for by somebody who knows all the facts and all the laws which govern them, what is the sense of saying that I can do what I want? Am I not a wholly, rigidly determined element in some block universe? Hegel thought that this perennial problem was one which he had solved. The world, according to him, as we have seen, is something which develops, now gradually and cumulatively, at other times by explosions. The forces whose conflicts create movement, whose final clashes are cataclysmic leaps into the next phase, take the form sometimes of institutions – Churches, States, cultures, legal systems – sometimes of great inventions, discoveries, artistic masterpieces, sometimes of individuals, groups, parties, personal relationships. This is the dialectical movement. But if I understand it, how can I oppose it? If I understand an art or a science – logic or music or mathematics – how can I want something which goes against it? To understand is not merely to accept, but actively to want what is understood, because to be understood is to become part of him who understands, part of his purposes, his goal and his development towards his goal. Of course, this is not an empirical hypothesis, not a scientific theory; no facts can falsify this Hegelian pattern. It is a vast metaphysical vision in which everything is accommodated either as a thesis or as an antithesis. Everything can be fitted in, nothing can be excluded, because every event and person and element in the world either accords or fails to accord with every other person, event and element – and whichever it does, it fits in either by being harmonious with something or by being in discord with it. There can be no evidence against such a view, for anything which might seem

contrary can be absorbed as the necessary element of contrariety.[1] For this reason it is not a scientific or rational explanation
in the sense in which, say, the Darwinian or Newtonian systems
are rational, because one could conceive of evidence against
them; they can be tested, but the dialectic cannot; it is a kind of
framework of things in general.

In this metaphysical vision, what happens to human freedom?
Hegel is very triumphant on this point. What is freedom but
doing what I wish to do, getting what I want to get, obtaining
from life what I am seeking for? I can only get this if I do not
run against the laws which govern the world. If I defy them I
shall be inevitably defeated. To wish to be something is the first
principle of rationality. It is irrational to wish to be annihilated,
to wish to cause a state of affairs in which there are no further
wishes, no further goals. If I want to do mathematics, it is self-
defeating to behave as if twice two did not make four. If I want
to build an aeroplane, it is suicidal to defy the laws of
aerodynamics. If I wish to be effective historically, I must not set
myself against the laws which govern human beings and institutions. This non-defiance is not an acquiescence which I consciously adopt with resignation, although I would rather be free.
To understand why things cannot be otherwise is to want them
not to be otherwise, because to understand things is to understand the reasons for them. To want things to be other than
what they rationally must be is to be mad. To want the universe
to be other than what it is, for Hegel, is like wanting twice two
to be seventeen. If the laws of history are assimilated into the
essence of my own thought, as the rules of arithmetic are, then
to want them otherwise is like wanting myself to be myself and
also different from what I am, to be guided by rules and not to
have them, to think and not to think. If you understand
Shakespeare, you cannot want Hamlet to have the character of
Falstaff, for that is not to understand Shakespeare's intentions,
not to understand why he created Hamlet and Falstaff as he did.

[1] As someone once remarked, facts which do not fit Hegel's hypothesis can
always be fitted into the category of what does not fit in, a special sort of
waste-paper basket category of the not-fitting.

To want Charlemagne to live after Louis XIV, and to think that Cromwell could well have lived in the nineteenth century, and Bismarck in the seventeenth, is not to understand how the world is made – to want a contradiction, to be irrational. Therefore I always want to be that which I am anyway forced to be; and to have what one wants is to be free. For everything to go as you want, for nothing ever to cross you, is absolute freedom, and the only thing which has that is the absolute spirit – everything there is. The world as a whole is totally free, and we are free to the extent to which we identify ourselves with the rational principles of the world. A free mathematician is a person who naturally thinks mathematically, and a man free in history is a man who naturally proceeds according to the rational laws which govern human lives, which govern history. To be happy, to be free, is to understand where one is and when one is; where one is on the map; and to act accordingly. If you do not act, you are acted upon, you become historical stuff, you become, as Seneca said, a slave dragged by the Fates, and not the wise man who is led by them. In Hegel, we do see history through the eyes of the victors, certainly not through the eyes of the victims. We see history in the way in which those who, in that sense, understood history have seen it; the Romans were victors, they won, and to win means to be on the right side of the historical flow. Perhaps the Cappadocians whom the Romans defeated thought very differently about things, understood the universe differently, but if they had understood it correctly they would not have been defeated, and because they were defeated they must have misunderstood it.

Therefore to understand things correctly, to be victorious, to survive, to be, in Hegel's sense of the word, real are in some way identified. Certainly history is full of crimes and tragedies from the point of view of a given generation. That is the way of the dialectic. History, says Hegel, is not a smooth progression, not the happy fields, the bubbling brooks of Rousseau's nature – that is a very false conception. History is the 'slaughter-bench', as he calls it, 'to which the happiness of peoples, the wisdom of States and the virtue of individuals have been brought as sacrifices'; 'history is not the theatre of happiness; periods of happiness are blank pages in it'. How is history made? It is made by the few, of course, and by human beings, who are the highest rational creatures. But it is not necessarily made by their conscious wishes and desires.

The great heroes of history, the people who occur at the climaxes, at the moments of synthesis, are people who may think that they are merely pursuing their own particular ends. Caesar, Alexander were ambitious men, and their principal desire was to aggrandise themselves, or to defeat their enemies, but history is wiser than they; history uses them, uses them semi-consciously, as its weapons. This Hegel calls 'the cunning of reason'. He says it is history that 'sets the passions to work for itself, while that which develops its being through such impulsion pays the penalty and suffers the loss'. In short there is a vast, single, all-embracing reason, or what he calls the spirit, the development of which is all that occurs. It is a development of the spirit because there exists nothing else; it is a self-development because nothing else can develop it. If we understand it we are its willing tool. If we do not understand it we struggle against it and are lost.

Not to like what you see to be rationally determined, to resist it, is mere suicidal mania, ultimate stupidity, a kind of un-grown-up-ness, a failure to be adult. 'Subjective' for Hegel is an extreme term of opprobrium. Who cares what a schoolboy thinks of the theory of Euclid or the propositions of Newton or of Einstein? To dislike the universe, to denounce it, to resist it, to find it not to your taste, to complain about it, to say that the facts are against you, that there is a brute mass of resistance to you which you cannot pierce, to be frustrated by this, to bleed as the result of falling upon the thorns of life – that is, for Hegel, a form of being inferior, being blind, not understanding, of stupidity and, ultimately, vice.

Let me try to explain this a little more clearly. For Hegel, understanding history is really understanding the nature of things in general, and that is why it is automatically a kind of conscious self-identification with their pattern, so that to be free and to be rational are the same; to be rational is to understand; to understand is to assimilate into one's own being; to be unfree means to be resisted by outward obstacles. When you have captured the obstacle it becomes yours, just as, when a piece of property is out of bounds to you, then by purchasing it, or by invading it, you make it yours and it is not out of bounds, and you are free.

There is something absurd and crazy, for Hegel, in praising or in condemning the vast process in terms of which everything is explicable. To be aware of the whole objective march of history, and then to praise some parts of it because we like them, and to condemn others because they may seem to contain cruelty or injustice or waste, is a mere indulgence in subjective moods. That is an inability to rise beyond what he calls 'civil society', constituted by the economic desires of men, the ordinary private desires of men for prosperity or comfort or a happy life, which is the level at which shallow thinkers like Locke remained. To see a vast human upheaval and then to condemn it because it is cruel or because it is unjust to the innocent is for Hegel profoundly foolish and contemptible. It is like condemning the fact that the number three has no rational square root. Who can wish to know what this or that man feels about events of cosmic importance? These dissatisfactions are trivial facts about some-one's passing feelings. To be truly worthy of the occasion is to rise to its level, to realise that something immense and critical is taking place, to have a sense of a historic occasion, when perhaps a new level is being attained by humanity which will automati-cally transform contemplation of both facts and systems of values.

In Hegel there is a great distinction, which runs through his entire work, between on the one hand the subjective, the emotional, the personal, the utilitarian, the middle-class, the individualistic, which may be a necessary stage in human development, but which is transient and by the early nineteenth century is certainly superseded; and on the other hand the objective, the demonstratively rational, the powerful, the inexor-able, the decisive, the concrete – what he calls 'the world-historical'. He is fascinated by the concept of a great man who is a maker and a breaker of societies, the being in whom for the moment history has concentrated her powerful and irresistible strength, who is at once an instrument and a goal of the remorseless march of history. For him, such questions as whether the great man, the earth-shaker, is good or virtuous or just are absolutely meaningless, and indeed petty, for the values implied by these words are themselves created and superseded by those very transformations of which the great man is the Herculean agent. For him the question of whether such a man is just or unjust belongs to the particular system of values, to the particular sphere of action, to the particular moment which is occurring in history at a given time. These are values which great men themselves have made in the past; but the martyrs of one generation are often the lawgivers of the next. Therefore to say that something is bad, wretched, wrong, monstrous, indignation-provoking in a given age is to say that it is so at the level which the great rational process has reached at that particular moment. But by the very transformation of that process by some immensely heroic act, by a revolution, by a war, by the appearance of some vast hero who alters the thoughts and acts of mankind, the values of the previous age become automatically superseded, and what seems abominable in one generation seems virtuous in the next. Therefore let us wait, for it is only what history will make real that is going to be valuable. A value, after all, if you want it to be real, must be objective, and 'objective' means that which the world – reason, the world pattern – intends, that which it supplies next in the irresistible development, the unrolling of the scroll, the inexorable march, what Hegel calls 'God's march through the universe', which for him ultimately is the activity of the State.

The pattern matters more than the individual. For what is the individual? The individual taken by himself is as unintelligible as would be a patch of colour, an isolated sound, a word divorced from the sentence of which it is a part, for words only make sense when combined in sentences, and colours and sounds, whether in nature or in art, when seen in the unique setting in which they in fact occur. Why should this be different in the case of human beings? There are no laws which apply to a man in isolation. I am what I am, because I am uniquely situated in the social setting of my time and place. I am connected by a myriad invisible threads to my fellow beings, to members of my family and my city, of my race and religion and country, to the living and the dead and those yet unborn. I am a kind of nodal point, the focus of an infinite number of strands which centre in, and radiate from, me and everyone else who enters with me into combinations and patterns, groups of lesser or greater tightness or looseness – the great society of the living and the dead of which Burke had spoken. To understand a man, you must understand his milieu, his friends and relations, his superiors and inferiors, what he does and what is done to him, and by what and by whom, not merely because this throws light on him, but because he literally does not exist except as part of this total pattern, any more than a sound in a tune exists (except in some uninteresting sense as a mere physical event) save as a particular ingredient of that particular tune, played on a particular instrument in the particular context in which the music is played. Hence Hegel's celebrated reduction of the individual to an abstract element of a 'concrete' social pattern; his denial that such patterns are mere arrangements of society, that the State and the laws are artificial devices designed for the convenience of individuals; and his insistence that they are networks of which the individuals, whether they will it or not, are the organically fused-together elements. Hence the celebration of the authority and the power and the greatness of the State as against the whims or individual inclinations of this or that citizen or subject.

There is no doubt much plausibility in the view advanced by Hegel's contemporaries, the historical jurists, who said that legal institutions are not so many arbitrary orders of kings or assemblies, or utilitarian devices consciously invented to procure this or that benefit for this or that person or class, but rather part of the unconscious or semi-conscious growth of societies, and expressive of their attitude to life, their half-articulate thoughts and wishes, their ideals and fears and hopes and beliefs and interests, at once the symbol and the substance of what they are and seem to themselves to be. Yet ultimately, driven to its extreme by Hegel, this view becomes a sinister mythology which authorises the indefinite sacrifice of individuals to such abstractions – for all that he calls them 'concrete' – as States, traditions, or the will or destiny of the nation or the race. The world is, after all, composed of things and persons and of nothing else. Societies or States are not things or persons, but ways in which things and persons are or come to be arranged; social patterns have no likes, no wills, no demands, no destinies, no powers. But Hegel does speak as if patterns, like States or Churches, are more real than people or things; as if it is not the houses that make the street, but the street that somehow creates the houses – which it does in a celebrated fairy tale by Hans Christian Andersen.

Among all the patterns the State is supreme. It is the highest of all the patterns because, like the iron ring of which Fichte spoke, it integrates them all; because it is humanity at its most self-conscious, at its most disciplined and its most orderly, and if we believe the universe to be a march, we must believe it to be marching in an intelligible direction, we must believe it to be a patterned order; and the State is the most ordered thing there is. Whatever resists it is bound to be annihilated. Rightly, because what is right and wrong is what history promotes or rejects. The sole objective source of right is the direction of the facts themselves, not individual judgement; not any particular code of laws, not any set of moral principles, but the imperative of history itself, the demands of history. There is in Hegel perpetual talk about what history demands and what history condemns, and the way we talk today about how such and such a nation or such and such a person has been condemned by history is a typical piece of Hegelian realism. This is the imagery and worship of power, of the movement of force for its own sake. This force is, for him, the divine process itself, crushing whatever is meant to be crushed, enthroning that whose hour to dominate has struck – and this, for Hegel, is the essence of the process. This is the source of Carlyle's heroes or Nietzsche's superman, of openly power-worshipping movements such as Marxism and Fascism, both of which (in their different ways) derived morality from historical success;[1] it is the source of the

---

[1] Marxism is a little more faithful to Hegel, perhaps, because it assumes that it is classes that exercise power, and class is a superhuman institution,

great contrast which Hegel is perpetually tracing between great men and ordinary human beings, between fighters who hack their way and raise humanity to a new level and the mere ants of the human anthill who perform their task without effectively questioning whether to carry such burdens is necessary. It survives in the distinction we still draw ourselves between (what we call) realistic and unrealistic. 'Realistic' often means harsh and brutal, not shrinking from what is usually considered immoral, not swayed by soft sentimental moral considerations.

Hegel is very strong about the necessity for violent action which may be condemned by the more prudish moralists in history. 'Gangrene', he says, 'is not cured with lavender water.' Progress is the work of heroes; heroes who stand above the conventional morality, because they embody the human spirit at its highest; at so high a level, at so mighty a pinnacle, that ordinary human beings can hardly discern what goes on at so lofty a height. They draw, he says, 'not from the peaceful time-hallowed tradition ... but from a spring whose contents are hidden, ... from an inner spirit still concealed beneath the surface'. Hence ordinary virtues do not apply here. Sometimes he grows sentimental about heroes: Alexander dies young, Caesar is assassinated, Napoleon is sent to St Helena. Sometimes he exults in their brutal strength. What he says about heroes, he also says about peoples. Peoples are always performing the enormous tasks which history places upon them, and when history has done with them, she rejects them. Peoples are like the garments which the great world-historical process now dons, now doffs, and casts about at will. Having quaffed the bitter draught of world history for which it yearned with infinite thirst, a people apprehends its purpose, and then it dies. A people which insists on surviving after its part is played is a mere political nullity and a bore.

History is a vast cataclysmic objective march, and those who do not obey it are wiped out by it. But why should we condone all these cruelties? Why should the mere fact of a thing having

whereas Fascists allow greater scope for the violent and imperious individual will.

happened in the way that it did automatically justify it? *Are* we so very much against the losers, the victims of history – against Don Quixote? Against the people who are crushed by the wheels of progress? Do we think it so wicked of Don Quixote to have protested against the vulgarity, the smallness, the immorality, the shoddiness of the facts, and to have tried however foolishly to erect a more noble ideal? Hegel does not burke this problem. For him the visions of the martyrs are not merely pathetic, not merely weak, not merely contemptible; for him they are vicious too, in a sense. The only thing which is bad is to resist the world process. For the world process is the incarnation of reason – when he says incarnation he means it in the literal sense – and to oppose it is immoral. Therefore he despises the utilitarians, the sentimentalists, the woolly, benevolent philanthropists, the people who want people to be happier, who wring their hands when they see the vast tragedies, the revolutions, the gas-chambers, the appalling suffering through which humanity goes. These persons are for him not merely contemptibly blind to the movement of history but positively immoral, because they resist that which is objectively good by pitting against it their subjective good; and subjective good is like subjective mathematics, it is absurd nonsense. It may obstruct the process for a little but it will be wiped out and pulverised.

Power alone is what Hegel celebrates in his dark, semi-poetical prose. There is a passage which makes this particularly clear. In 1806 Hegel was looking over the last pages of his first great contribution, the *Phenomenology of Spirit*. He was living in Jena at that time and saw the camp-fires of the French on the eve of the great battle of that name. It suddenly dawned upon him that there it was – history in its objectivity. Still more did he think so when he saw Napoleon riding through the city a few days later. He said, 'the Emperor – that world soul – I saw him ride through the town ... It is really an odd feeling to see such a personality physically concentrated in a unique point of space, seated on horseback, while his imperious thought roams and radiates over the entire world' – a vast mind, vast strength, a great bully crushing men and things with its mailed fist. This is Hegel's conception of objective history.

What is one to say about this? One can only say that this curious identification of what is good and what is successful is precisely what the average human being rejects. It is not what we mean by the good and the right. It is impossible to say to us that merely to pit oneself against superior force is in itself immoral. Hegel does not think it is immoral if you are ultimately going to win, if the martyr of today is the hero and the lawgiver and the dictator of tomorrow; but he thinks that to be good and to be successful, in the ultimate, vast, world-historical sense, are identical. This kind of political pragmatism, this kind of success-worship, revolts our normal moral feelings; and there is no genuine argument in Hegel which is really effective against that revulsion. It is merely that in Hegel's vision there is a vast coherent spectacle of history, with which he identifies his own worship of what are for him true values. True values for him are those which are effective; history is the big battalions, marching down a broad avenue, with all the unfulfilled possibilities, all the martyrs and visionaries, wiped out; and morality is really a specific form of bowing before the facts. This identification of what works with what is good, of what is right with what succeeds, with that which crushes resistance, with that which deserves to crush resistance – this is the sure hallmark of the Hegelian system, whenever it is applied to politics. An unsuccessful rebellion is always bad. That is why it is not perhaps very surprising that he should have approved of the censorship decrees by which Metternich controlled the right to free speech in German universities, nor that he should have been sent for to Berlin by the King of Prussia, who certainly had no desire for any liberal in that particular post at that particular time.

Yet we must not be unfair to Hegel. He did a very great deal for the advance of civilisation. Almost single-handed he created institutional history. Although Herder and even Vico had adumbrated it, it was Hegel who impressed this truth vividly upon the imagination of his generation: that human history was the history of institutions at least as much as the history of kings, generals, adventurers, conquerors, lawgivers. Moreover it was really he who made it plain that what people looked for in history was the individual and the unique, not the general, and that in this respect history was deeply and genuinely different from the natural sciences. Hegel's remarks on the natural sciences are often ludicrous – both ignorant and grotesquely dogmatic. But he did show great insight in conveying the idea that the natural sciences always search for that which is common to all the objects under observation, so that by finding what is uniform in many different things, atoms, tables, elephants, earthquakes, they can formulate laws which apply to an infinite number of similar instances of atoms, tables and the rest. Yet this is the last thing that one seeks from history. When I read about Robespierre or Napoleon, I do not wish to be told what it is that Napoleon had in common with all other adventurers or with all other emperors; I do not wish to know exactly how Robespierre resembled all other lawyers and revolutionaries. What I wish to discover is that which is uniquely important about and characteristic of these two men. I want Robespierre and his life and character and acts 'brought to life' before me in their unique individuality. When I read about the French Revolution or the Renaissance, I am only interested in a minor way in what these great episodes of human civilisation had in common with developments in Babylon or among the Aztecs. This may be of interest to sociologists, it may indeed be intrinsically illuminating, but the business of historians is to convey differences more than similarities, to paint a portrait of a unique, absolutely specific set of events and persons – a portrait and not an X-ray. Hegel applied this notion to institutions as well as to individuals. Certainly nobody before the nineteenth century conceived it possible to write the biography of an army, of a civil service, of a religious development. Hegel's treatment of history as if it were the self-development of a vast and infinite world spirit contributed greatly, for all its mythology and darkness, to the rise of a new history, the history of the interconnection of all things. Perhaps Hegel's most original achievement was to invent the very idea of the history of thought: for certainly nobody before him had written, or conceived it possible to write, the history of

philosophical or any other thought, not as a loose succession –
first one sage and his system, then another – but as a continuous
development of ideas from one generation of thinkers to the
next, and intimately related to economic or social or other kinds
of changes in a society or culture. All this is now so much taken
for granted that Hegel's originality can scarcely be realised
today.

Moreover, Hegel seemed to place immense stress on history
and the value of history, and the fact that everything in it matters
and nothing else matters at all. More emphatically even than
Herder he spoke as if facts could not be clearly distinguished
into the historically relevant and irrelevant; since the way in
which people wear their clothes or eat their food, sail the seas or
sing their songs, their handwriting, their accent, may be more
illuminating than many of their more official acts – their wars,
their treaties, their constitutions. There is no telling what may
not be useful towards explaining the total process of history, in
which this or that people played its part, appeared on the stage at
its destined moment and duly left it after its hour had struck.

Hegel's attack upon the old moralising history which looked
to the past mainly to learn about errors and vices, his condemna-
tion of blame and praise, his invitation to rational men to
identify themselves with the great moving forces as such, while
they may have led to the worship of power, to a peculiarly
brutal form of political realism, did also contribute to making all
historical facts appear of equal and incalculable value. For the
solution to all questions now seemed to lie in history – a priori
history, it is true, and spiritual history, but still history. History
was now as important in telling men how to live as theology
once was. It was the new theodicy – the interpretation of the
ways of God to men. And in this way it discredited eighteenth-
century history, which classified facts in terms of some subjective criterion of good and bad, and it weighed the scales in
favour of that scrupulous factual history which treated all facts
as being on the same level, and was prepared to look for them in
the most unlikely corners. History was supremely important;
everything in it deserved notice, for it might throw light by

laying bare the essence of that unique network, that concatenation of elements which forms the individual personality, in this case the universe, of which men are elements and limbs.

Furthermore, Hegel drew attention to unconscious factors in history: the dark forces, the vast impersonal urges, what he liked to think of as the semi-conscious strivings of reason seeking to realise its being, but which we may call simply the half-unconscious forces, the occult psychological causes which we now think at least as important as the conscious intentions of generals or kings or violent revolutionaries. This too helped to de-personalise and, if I may put it so, de-moralise history.

There is a further respect in which Hegel's method is valuable, namely in its application to works of art, to the sense of artistic greatness and beauty, and to the aesthetic field generally. He thought he was reducing the confused language of the romantics to something disciplined and rigorous. This was an illusion. The form acquired a specious kind of technicality but the content remained thoroughly dark. Despite all his efforts the concepts remain loose. All the romantic terminology which he and other German metaphysicians and poets of this period employed – the notions of transcendence and integration, of inner conflict, of forces which at once destroy and fuse with and fertilise each other; the notion of a unity which is at once the purpose and the principle, the pattern and the goal, and the essence of something which is at the same time an entity and a process, a being and a becoming – all this, which has led to such vagueness, and often nonsense, when applied in logic or history or the sciences, has a unique part to play in describing the indescribable: beautiful objects, psychical processes, works of art. Romantic terminology generally is best at describing not easily analysable experiences precisely because it is evocative, imprecise, indefinite, and has a rich vagueness of association and a rich use of imagery and metaphor. How are we to describe a poem, a symphony, an aesthetic experience of almost any kind? Perhaps it is best to say nothing: but if we wish to speak, then the lucid, intelligible public language used by really clear elegant thinkers such as Hume and Voltaire, or even Helvétius, is of little use here. In music, for example, it does sometimes make a kind of sense to speak of a dialectical growth – a tune which clashes with and flows into other musical phrases, leading to their mutual annihilation and yet not: also to their transcendence, to the integration of the conflicting forces into something richer and, if you like, higher, more perfect than the original ingredients. Here one can speak of the obscure semi-conscious growth of forces which burst out suddenly in some splendid, golden shower. The turbid and infinitely suggestive language of Hegel, and still more of other romantic philosophers, of Schelling, the brothers Schlegel, Novalis, and indeed of Coleridge and to some degree of Carlyle, really does at moments penetrate by its use of musical and biological imagery to something like the heart of the creative process. Such language can do something to convey the essence of what the development of a pattern is like, the impalpable yet very real interrelation of sounds and feeling – and even moral purposes – in a symphony, or an opera, or a mass; and with a greater risk of clouding the issue, such a semi-poetical way of talking may give a far more vivid sense of the contours of a culture, of the ideals of a school of artists or philosophers, the attitude of a generation – something not to be analysed by the more precise, more logically coherent, more tough-minded terminology which alone, with its standards of integrity and scholarship, guarantees truth and clarity in fields amenable to more exact treatment. In literary criticism and in the history of art, in the history of ideas and the analysis of civilisation, in every discipline in which there is poetry as well as prose, the Hegelian prescription – the thesis–antithesis method, the description of everything as perpetually passing into its opposite, as an unstable equilibrium of mutually conflicting forces – genuinely transformed both the European sensibility and its modes of expression.

Hegel's real error was to suppose that the whole of the universe – everything – was a kind of work of art which was creating itself, and therefore that this kind of half-biological, half-musical terminology was what described it best. As a result he imposed upon mankind a great many erroneous views; for example, that values were identical with facts, and that what was good was what was successful – which all morally sensitive persons, long before and after his day, have rejected, and rightly rejected. His great crime was to have created an enormous mythology in which the State is a person, and history is a person, and there is the one single pattern which metaphysical insight alone can discern. He created a school of a priori history which ignored the ordinary facts because the philosopher, armed with superior insight, can deduce what happens by a species of rational double vision, a kind of clairvoyance which enables him to tell in a mathematically certain way what has occurred, as opposed to the sadly empirical, imperfect, fussy way in which the ordinary historian has to proceed.

In spite of all his vices Hegel created an immense system which for a long time dominated the minds of mankind. As for liberty, there can be none in a tight pattern. There can be no liberty where obedience to the pattern is the only true self-expression, where what you call liberty is not the possibility of acting within some kind of vacuum, however small, which is left for your own personal choice, in which you are not interfered with by others. Hegelian liberty simply consists of conquest or possession of that which obstructs you, until you have conquered and possessed everything, and then you are identical with the master of the universe. Until you have done that, the best that you can do is to try to understand why you must be as you must be, and instead of groaning and moaning and complaining about the appalling burdens upon you, welcome them joyously. But the joyous welcome of burdens is not liberty.

There have always been people who have wanted to be secure in some tight establishment, to find their rightful secure place in some rigid system, rather than to be free. To such people Hegel says a word of comfort. Nevertheless, fundamentally this is a vast confusion, a historically fatal identification of liberty, as we understand it, with security – the sense of belonging to some unique place where you are protected against obstacles because you can foresee them all. But that is not what we call liberty: maybe it is a form of wisdom, of understanding, of loyalty, of happiness, of holiness. The essence of liberty has always lain in the ability to choose as you wish to choose, because you wish so to choose, uncoerced, unbullied, not swallowed up in some vast system; and in the right to resist, to be unpopular, to stand up for your convictions merely because they are your convictions. That is true freedom, and without it there is neither freedom of any kind, nor even the illusion of it.

SAINT-SIMON

COMTE HENRI DE SAINT-SIMON is the greatest of all the prophets of the twentieth century. His writings and his life were confused and even chaotic. He was regarded in his own lifetime as an inspired lunatic. He wrote badly – with flashes of intuition mingled with immense tracts of naïve and fantastic imagining. His reputation grew posthumously. The fact that Karl Marx, who borrowed so much from him, relegated him to the ranks of Utopian socialists, so called, did a great deal to create the impression that, although a gifted man, he was too naïve and too foolish and too monomaniacal to be worth close study. Yet if prophecy is laid along prophecy and the predictions of Karl Marx are compared to those of Saint-Simon, the balance will turn out to be more than favourable to Saint-Simon.

All his life, Saint-Simon was possessed with the idea that he was the great new Messiah who had at last come to save the earth, and he lived at a time when a great many people were under that peculiar impression. There never was a period to compare with the end of the eighteenth and the beginning of the nineteenth century for the extraordinary density of megalomaniac Messiahs. Everybody at that period seemed to think that he at last had been gifted with that unique power of penetration and imagination which was destined to solve all human evils. If you read Rousseau, you get the impression that although he thinks he has predecessors it is only he to whom the final light has been vouchsafed. Similarly with Fichte: you feel that he is saying that, although naturally Luther was important and Christ was important, and the great Greek philosophers were important, yet the final illumination may be obtained only from him –

that it is his mission, his dedication, to open to humanity those gates which no doubt have been prised half or a quarter open by previous thinkers, but which it was his privilege to fling open finally and for ever.

You get exactly the same impression when you read Hegel, who felt that he was the summation, the complete synthesis, of all the thought that had gone before, finally, in an immense harmonious composition which at last was the sum of all human wisdom, of all human knowledge, so that, after him, all that his disciples, and indeed humanity, would have to do was simply to work out the results and apply them. Similarly in France, with the so-called Utopian socialists, Saint-Simon, Fourier and even their successors Bazard and Leroux, you get the impression that they say: 'Well, of course, there are predecessors; there was Moses, there was Socrates, there was Christ, there was Newton, or Descartes, or other important thinkers, even geniuses. But all these people merely adumbrated, they merely hinted; they merely obtained a corner of the truth. The final revelation is what I now have to say to you.' In spite of that, Saint-Simon remains an important, and indeed marvellous, thinker.

Let me try to enumerate some of the doctrines of which he was as much an originator as anyone. It is very difficult ever to attribute a doctrine or an idea to one person and one person only in so inexact a subject as the humane sciences. Nevertheless, one can without great fear of contradiction say that Saint-Simon is the father of European historicism far more than the Germans; that he is the person who really criticised the unhistorical methods of the eighteenth century and put forward an interpretation of history of his own which was at the root of the great French historical school of the early nineteenth century, and which really provided those weapons in terms of which concrete history came to be written, rather than those much more shadowy ideological schemata which the German idealists provided at the same time.

He is not only the father of historical writing – at any rate in France, and arguably in Western Europe. He is also the father of what I should like to call the technological interpretation of

history. This is not quite the same as the materialistic interpretation of history which we associate with the name of Marx, but it
does lie at its root, and in certain respects is a much more
original and tenable view. Saint-Simon is the first person to
define classes in the modern sense, as economic social entities,
dependent in a direct way upon the progress of technology – the
progress of machinery, the progress of the ways in which people
obtain and distribute and consume products. In short, he is the
first person to draw serious attention to the economic factors in
history. Moreover, wherever there is talk about a planned
society, about a planned economy, about technocracy, about the
necessity for what the French call *dirigisme*, anti-*laissez-faire*;
wherever there is a New Deal; wherever there is propaganda in
favour of some kind of rational organisation of industry and of
commerce, in favour of applying science for the benefit of
society, and, in general, in favour of everything which we have
now come to associate with a planned rather than a *laissez-faire*
State – wherever there is talk of this sort, the ideas which are
bandied saw the light originally in the half-published manu-
scripts of Saint-Simon.

Again, Saint-Simon more than anyone else invented the
notion of the government of society by élites, using a double
morality. There is of course something of that in Plato and in
previous thinkers, but Saint-Simon is almost the first thinker
who comes out and says that it is important for society to be
governed not democratically, but by élites of persons who
understand the technological needs and the technological possibilities of their time; and that, since the majority of human
beings are stupid, and since they mostly obey their emotions,
what the enlightened élite must do is to practise one morality
themselves and feed their flock of human subjects with another.
So the notion of the double morality, of which we have heard so
much in, for example, the hideous Utopias of Aldous Huxley or
Orwell, has its origin in the golden, optimistic view of Saint-
Simon, who, so far from thinking such a double standard
immoral or dangerous, thinks that it is the only way to progress,
to advance humanity towards the gate of that paradise which, in
common with the thinkers of the eighteenth century, he thinks it

best deserves and is on the point of attaining – if only it will listen to his views.

He is one of the most trenchant attackers of such eighteenth-century shibboleths as civil liberty, human rights, natural rights, democracy, *laissez-faire*, individualism, nationalism. He attacks them because he is the first person to see – as the thinkers of the eighteenth century never did quite clearly see – the incompatibility between the view that wise men ought to direct society and the view that people ought to govern themselves; the incompatibility, in short, between a society which is directed by a group of wise men who alone know towards what goal to move and how to get humanity to move towards it, and the notion that it is better to govern oneself, even than to be governed well. He chooses, of course, in favour of good government. But he is perfectly aware that this means the impossibility of self-government. He is the first person to make that clear, and that is why his attack on all the cherished liberal ideas of the eighteenth century, and indeed of the nineteenth and twentieth centuries, has not only a modern ring, but something truly original about it. It is as if he were the first person to feel the logical consequences of the beliefs which seem to be held so comfortably together with their opposites in the far shallower and apparently far clearer thought of the great thinkers of the eighteenth century, both in France and in Germany.

Finally, Saint-Simon is the first originator of what might be called secular religions – that is to say, the first person to see that one cannot live by technological wisdom alone; that something must be done to stimulate the feelings, the emotions, the religious instincts of mankind. He is the first person – not cold-bloodedly, because he did it with a great deal of enthusiasm and warmth, which were natural to him – to invent that substitute for religion, that secularised, humanised, de-theologicalised variant of Christianity of which so many versions began to circulate in the nineteenth century and after – something like the religion of humanity of Kant; something like all the pseudo-religions, all the moralities with a faint religious flavour, which were regarded as a substitute, for rational men, for the blindly dogmatic and anti-scientific theological darkness of the past. That alone gives

Saint-Simon a claim to be regarded as one of the most seminal, one of the most original, and one of the most influential thinkers – if not the most influential thinker – of our own day; and like other thinkers whom I have been discussing, he is more relevant to our own century than he was to the nineteenth, as I propose to show.

Let us begin with the notion of historicism, for which, as I say, he was largely responsible. The problem which occupied Saint-Simon and his contemporaries was the failure of the French Revolution. Saint-Simon was born in 1760 and died in 1825, and I ought to say something about his life in order to explain how his views came to be what they were. He was a member of the great family of Saint-Simon, which had produced, about a hundred years before, the famous Duke, the author of the *Mémoires*, and he was very proud of that. He even traced his descent from Charlemagne. Let me quote him on the subject:

> I write because I have new ideas. I express them in the form in which they have taken shape in my mind. I leave it to professional writers to polish them. I write as a gentleman, as a descendant of the Counts of Vermandois, and as the literary heir of the Duke of Saint-Simon. All the great things that were ever done and said were done and said by gentlemen: Copernicus, Galileo, Bacon, Descartes, Newton, Leibniz – they were all members of the gentry. Napoleon too would have written down all his ideas instead of practising them, had he not happened upon a vacant throne.

This is a fair example of Saint-Simon's bombastic style. It was said that he got his valet to wake him every morning with the words: 'Rise, M. le Comte – you have great things to achieve.'

When he was a young man, being of a restless disposition and imaginative temperament and warm heart, he went to America, where he entered into American service and took part in the siege of Yorktown under General Washington. After the American War of Liberation he went down to Mexico, where, being already possessed by ideas of the necessity of reforming society by vast technological schemes, he tried to persuade the Spanish Viceroy of Mexico to pierce the Isthmus of Panama and dig a canal, which he thought would revolutionise trade in those waters. At that time the idea was very premature and nobody took the slightest notice of it. From there he went to Holland, where he tried to stimulate an attack on British colonies; from there to Spain, where he tried to get a canal dug between Madrid and the sea. He was preoccupied with the notion of making nature serve mankind, getting something for nothing – getting a canal dug and then letting the water, nature herself, perform the work which was so laboriously and so wastefully performed by human beings. None of this came about; indeed the Spanish canal, which nearly went through, was overwhelmed by the French Revolution.

In the Revolution, of course, he sympathised most warmly with the reformers. He had been a pupil of the great mathematician and essayist, the editor of the Encyclopaedia, d'Alembert. He knew some of the Encyclopaedists of the end of the eighteenth century quite well personally and he was, at that time, set to complete the cycle of the century's enlightened men. He needed to drop the title of Count, and he called himself Monsieur Bonhomme. He took part in the Revolution on the side of the rebels, of the Gironde. Presently the Revolution developed into the Terror, and Saint-Simon, as an aristocrat, was almost arrested – a warrant went out in his name. Somebody else was arrested by mistake and Saint-Simon, very characteristically, as soon as he learnt this, gave himself up in order to liberate the man who was innocently incarcerated. He miraculously survived the Terror, and when he emerged threw himself with undiminished zeal into the stream of life, his great theory being that he wanted to reform humanity. Something was obviously gravely wrong with the affairs of men if all these admirable ideas conceived by men of such high character and such omniscience, such exquisite wit and such penetrating intelligence, such scrupulous attention to the truth, nevertheless ended in the slaughter of the guillotine. But in order to reform mankind one must know, one must learn, one must study all the sciences and all the arts; and more than that, one must quaff the cup of experience, one must understand the true nature of virtue and of vice, and in order to do that one must have as many and as varied experiences as possible. One must touch life at as many points as possible. In short, one must live. In order to do this one must have money. But Saint-Simon's estate had been sequestrated by the Revolution. Consequently, he threw himself into financial speculation, took part in the sales of the confiscated estates of the nobility, made an enormous fortune, was cheated out of it by his German partner Baron Redern, and ended as he had begun in the Revolution – penniless.

By this time he had lived. He had given enormous dinner parties to which he invited those he regarded as the most interesting men of the time – the physicists, the chemists, the physiologists, the mathematicians – from all of whom he hoped to learn about the secrets of their craft. Some mathematics he already knew through d'Alembert. He complained in later life that these scientists consumed his food and talked about everything under the sun except the sciences about which he wished to question them. Nevertheless he did pick up, here and there, fragments of this and that, and became a typical imaginative autodidact. His head was a perpetual buzz of the most extraordinary confusion and chaos. In his writings the ideas of the greatest depth and brilliance alternate with absolute nonsense. You begin, for example, reading an early treatise about the freedom of the seas, about which he had political theories, and suddenly, without knowing where you are, you find that you are in the midst of a disquisition on gravitation, and not just on gravitation in Newton's sense, but a quite mystical gravitation which affects the intellectual as well as the physical sphere. You think that you are reading about historical facts of the Middle Ages and you are suddenly told that humanity is like a single man – an idea already found in Pascal – and then that the age of mankind today is about forty – between thirty-five and forty-five – and in another place that the age of the French people is about twenty-one. You read pages of the greatest interest about his views on the development of mankind in the classical age and into the Christian Middle Ages, and suddenly you are told that Homer, who invented polytheism, also invented democracy, because there was democracy on Olympus, and that is how there came to be democracy on earth.

But let us leave out all the fantastic, naïve and the ludicrous aspects of Saint-Simon. His hypothesis about why the French Revolution had failed was perhaps the most original by then put forward. Everyone had explained the disaster in accordance with his own views. Why did the Revolution fail? The liberals said, because of the Terror, in other words, because the Revolutionaries were not liberal enough – did not respect human rights sufficiently. The orthodox and religious and conservatives said, because men had broken away from tradition, or from the word of God, and the spirit of God was sent to visit those who had preferred their own unaided human reason to the divine faith. The socialist fanatics – people like Babeuf – said, because the Revolution had not gone far enough, because equal distribution of property ought to have occurred, because, in short, though there may have been liberty, that liberty was nothing without economic equality. Many other explanations were also put forward. Saint-Simon's explanation in a sense resembled Hegel's explanation, but was infinitely more concrete, infinitely more to do with actual living human beings and real history as opposed to the vast shadowy metaphysical ideas, like the shadows of a great Gothic cathedral, in which Hegel seemed permanently to dwell. Saint-Simon said this was because he was not understood, and in his early writings he begins to put forward his own view of what history is. He is really the father of the quasi-materialist explanation, as I said before. For him, history is a story of living men trying to develop their faculties as richly and many-sidedly as possible. In order to do this, they exploit nature; in order to exploit nature, they have to have tools or weapons. Consequently their imagination, their inventiveness, everything that they have with which to think and to will, is directed upon the discovery of the optimum weapons for the subjugation of nature and the procuring to themselves of what will satisfy their desires, their inclinations and what he likes to call their interests.

The very invention of weapons in this way creates what is called technological advance, and the technological advance itself creates classes. It creates classes because the people who have the weapons can dominate those who have not. This very simple, basic idea Marx borrowed from Saint-Simon, if not totally, then certainly more than from anyone else. Once you have a class association on the part of the able, the gifted, the superior, who have invented tools and weapons by which they can procure more, by which they can extract more from nature than others, the others gradually find themselves dominated by this superior élite. They are not dominated for long, because ultimately they become rebellious, they become discontented, they think that they too, if only they allowed their imaginations and their reasons to work, can invent something with which they can not only get more from nature than they are getting, but perhaps overthrow the élite. The élite gradually, as with all élites, becomes obsolete, their ideas become ossified, they do not realise that invention and discovery are going on underneath them, among the lower class; and gradually, because they cling for too long to weapons of production (if one can speak in such terms), or anyhow to economic forms of life which are no longer suitable to the new weapons, to the new technological advances which the recalcitrant, indignant, active, imaginative, ambitious slaves are in the meanwhile perfecting, they are duly overthrown by this lower class, which itself then comes to power, only gradually to be ousted and made obsolete by the persons whom they exploit, whom they use.

In a way this looks exactly like the Marxist, materialist view of history, but Saint-Simon does not say what Marx says, namely, that all ideas are dominated by the conditions of distribution or production, by economic factors. He does think ideas are born only at the time when they satisfy an interest. In that sense people make inventions and discoveries, and think thoughts, and invent mathematics or poetry or whatever it may be, only in response to the general conditions of their time – only when this kind of thing satisfies their particular impulses, which are themselves conditioned to some degree by the economic environment and by the way in which people live. But he thinks that these ideas have a vast independent influence far greater than Marxists accord them, and therefore he thinks that inventions are as much the products of ideas, and in particular that classes are as much the products of ideas, as they are of technological evolution as such. For example, he thinks that slavery is an idea which was born at a certain period when people realised they would have much more leisure if they could make slaves do their work; similarly, the abolition of slavery was not so much the result of the pressure of economic circumstances, because it had become uneconomic to use slaves, which is the typical Marxist interpretation of this event, but because of the rise of Christianity. Christianity itself may have something to do with the economic world in which it was born; nevertheless it was Christian ideas – which were primarily religious, spiritual, ethical – that actually abolished slavery, when it need not have been abolished but for the birth of these ideas. Hence Saint-Simon's tremendous emphasis on the role of genius in history, on the fact that unless there are men of genius and unless they are given an opportunity of functioning, unless, in short, the great ideas of great men who perceive and understand the circumstances of their own time with a deeper insight and greater imagination are given scope, progress will be retarded. Progress is by no means automatic, by no means depends on some kind of inevitable machinery of the clash of classes or technological advance.

From this he developed the notion that history must be understood as a kind of evolution of mankind in the satisfaction of its various needs, and for that reason where the needs are different the satisfaction will be different. Therefore the dogmatic judgements which the eighteenth century was so fond of passing upon the Middle Ages or upon earlier periods as periods of darkness, ignorance, prejudice, superstition, ages of emptiness, and indeed contemptible and detestable in comparison with the dawning light of the rationalism of the eighteenth century – that was a profoundly unhistorical and totally untenable view.

Everything must be judged in its proper context. This idea, so familiar to us now, so simple, was not at all familiar to the people of the beginning of the nineteenth century. Everything must be judged in its context: Saint-Simon makes this idea much clearer than Herder. The Middle Ages, which we call dark, were not dark to themselves. The Middle Ages were a period when human needs were very different from ours, and an age ought to be approved of or disapproved of, praised or blamed, thought great or small, progressive or reactionary, in accordance with whether it satisfied the needs of its time, not the needs of some later period completely alien to its own time. Saint-Simon says: We always hear about this idea of progress, but what are we told about what progress is? What is this inevitable progress by which the eighteenth century is better than the seventeenth, and the seventeenth better than the sixteenth, and the sixteenth better than all the preceding ages? We are told that it is because men learn from nature, and because men apply reason, and something about more being done for the common good – but these, he says, are very vague terms; we do not know what people mean by reason, what they mean by nature. Let me give you some criteria for progress, he says, which will be concrete and which we may be able to use in writing history properly. He is as good as his word. He gives four criteria of progress, and very interesting they are.

The first is this: The progressive society is that which provides the maximum means of satisfying the greatest number of needs of the human beings who compose it. Anything is progressive which does this, which satisfies the maximum number of needs – that is the central idea of Saint-Simon from the beginning to the end. Human beings have certain needs – not necessarily for happiness, not necessarily for wisdom, for knowledge, for self-sacrifice or whatever it may be – and what they want is to satisfy them. These needs should be indulged, without asking why, and anything which gives a rich and many-sided development to these needs, which assists the greatest growth of personality in as many directions as is possible, that is progress or progressive.

The second criterion is this: Anything that is progressive will give the opportunity to the best to reach the top. The best, for him, are the most gifted, the most imaginative, the cleverest, the most profound, the most energetic, the most active, those who want the full flavour of life. For Saint-Simon there are very few classes of men: those who enhance life and those who are against it, those who want to get things done and want to provide things for people – who want a thing to happen, who want to satisfy needs – and those who are in favour of lowering the tone, making things quieter, allowing things to sink, who are against all the bustle, who want things, on the whole, to descend, decline and ultimately approach the condition of complete nullity.

The third criterion of progress is the provision of the maximum unity and strength for the purpose of a rebellion or an invasion; and the fourth criterion is conduciveness to invention and discovery and civilisation. For example, leisure conduces to these, and that is why slavery was seen, in his own time, as a progressive institution – or the invention of writing, or whatever it may be.

These are concrete criteria and, Saint-Simon says, if you judge history in terms of these the picture changes very deeply from that which has been presented to us by the dogmatists of the eighteenth-century Enlightenment. The dark ages cease to be dark if you think of what, for example, Pope Gregory VII or St Louis did in their day. These men, after all, built roads, they drained marshes. They built hospitals, they taught vast numbers of men to read and to write. Above all, they preserved the unity of Europe, they held back the invaders of the East, they civilised sixty million people, and sixty million people lived in a unitary manner, under roughly the same regime, and were able to develop harmoniously together. This is by no means a dark age; this is an age far less broken, far less turbid, far less frustrated for those who lived in it than the ages which followed. An age is progressive in which the largest number of people can do as much of what they want at that particular moment as is possible for them. The so-called dark ages were a period of the richest possible development of mankind at that time and in that condition of technological advance. Of course, all these things pass, these institutions become obsolete, because they are super-seded. New inventions occur, new discoveries are made, new men of genius arrive who automatically, by stirring people's minds, create new needs. The old institutions cannot satisfy the new needs, or become vested interests; they press against those needs, they try to repress them, restrain them, stop them, and they become a drag upon progress. Ultimately they become obsolescent, and somebody arises who destroys them, throws them over. That is a revolution. A revolution always means that somebody or other must arise for the purpose of clearing out what has become a completely antiquated, no longer useful institution which has outlived any possible good which it might conceivably once have done. Therefore history for Saint-Simon is a kind of rhythm of what his disciples called organic and critical periods. Organic periods are periods when humanity is unified, when it develops harmoniously, when the people who are in charge of it on the whole foster progress – progress in the sense of providing the maximum number of people with the maximum of opportunities for satisfying the maximum number of their needs, whatever they are. Critical periods are periods when these arrangements are becoming obsolescent, when the institutions themselves become obstacles to progress, when human beings feel that what they want is different from that which they are getting, when there is a new spirit which is about to sunder the old bottles in which it is still imprisoned – when, for example, as Saint-Simon thought of his own day, we have an industrial age which is still ludicrously and artificially confined within obsolete feudal frameworks.

The critical age is an age when destruction predominates over construction. It is something inferior in Saint-Simon's eyes, but nevertheless it is inevitable and necessary. For example, in his discussion of the eighteenth century and what made the French Revolution he says the French Revolution was really made by lawyers and metaphysicians. These are fundamentally destroyers. What do lawyers do? Lawyers employ such concepts as absolute rights, natural rights and liberty, and liberty is always a negative concept. The invocation of liberty means that somebody is trying to take something away from you which you then try to invent some reason for keeping. In short, a situation has arisen in which humanity, or the greater part of it, does not have enough to live by, and you feel hemmed in, you feel repressed. So you engage professionals called lawyers, or professionals called metaphysicians, for the purpose of doing something which you cannot do yourself, namely somehow or other to extract out of the ruling class something which you are too weak to force them to deliver by sheer violence on your own part. So lawyers are people who are engaged in inventing good and bad reasons for circumventing the old, worn-out machinery of government, the old obsolete tradition which is stifling vast sections of the population; and metaphysicians are people, particularly in the eighteenth century, who perform the very necessary task of undermining the old religions. Christianity, says Saint-Simon, was a great thing in its own day, as was Judaism, but it must develop, it must advance. If it remains static, it will burst, it will be overthrown. That is why, of all the great religious reformers, he dislikes Luther the most. Luther to him is a man too riveted to his particular faith, which was no doubt necessary for the purpose of overthrowing Catholicism, which Saint-Simon thought was becoming somewhat old-fashioned, obsolete, oppressive in Luther's day. For that Luther substituted devotion to the Bible, a single book. No doubt the Bible was all very well for a semi-nomadic Jewish tribe living in a small country in the eastern Mediterranean, but it cannot cope with the development of nations. Flexibility is wanted, perpetual change, perpetual advance. The Roman Church, whatever may be said against it, has a flexible element. No doubt it is reactionary in some ways, repressive and oppressive in others, but by means of endless legal fictions, by asserting that the source of authority is not an unalterable printed text but an altering human institution, which after all consists of generations of men, each of which is a little different from those of the past, it made itself sufficiently flexible to be able to guide humanity through the Middle Ages with immense success. This is precisely what Luther put an end to. He broke the European unity, he tied religion to something unaltering, he asserted private, absolute principles. If there is anything which Saint-Simon detests it is the notion of absolute principle – nothing is stable, nothing is absolute, everything evolves, everything responds to the movement of the times, to the evolution of humanity, to the new inventions, new discoveries, new minds, new souls, new hearts which it is gradually producing. Consequently he is on the whole pro-Catholic and anti-Protestant; but towards the end he is not an orthodox Christian at all.

As for the French Revolution, what was that? That was

simply a revolution which occurred at the end of a period of long elaboration. The development of industry and commerce, and economic changes of a very violent and upsetting kind, had been occurring since at any rate the beginning of the seventeenth century. Too little notice had been taken of this by those whose business it was to govern mankind. Duly, as a result of mismanagement on the part of people who lived in the traditional past and did not understand that a new industrial age was dawning or that the middle classes were now the persons with the real power (and Saint-Simon is nowhere more eloquent or more penetrating than when he is discussing what he means by real power, and the people who really win it), the French government, like those of other nations, did not proceed in accordance with these changes, did not shift their arrangements accordingly. Consequently the Treasury had gone bankrupt when they called upon the State to assist them. The Third Estate, in whose hands by this time the real power was, though it did not know it, suddenly realised that it did not need to compromise. It had the power: all it had to do was to use it. Why should they pay for what they could take? Why should they use persuasion when they could use force? And the Revolution occurred.

In short, Saint-Simon interprets the Revolution as the rising of the middle class to class-consciousness, consciousness of its real place and the fact that it could satisfy its demands by simply blowing away the few simple rules, the completely hollowed-out earlier classes – the clergy and the aristocracy and the army – which had been sitting on their shoulders, suppressing them, with no *raison d'être* that applied in the new world. And the lawyers, what part had they played? They supplied arguments, slogans to the new bourgeoisie; but any slogans become obsolete in time, and their slogans – 'All Power for the People', 'Human Liberty' and so forth – were just as hollow as the slogans of the reactionaries whom they opposed. No doubt they performed a very necessary task, the task of termites, in boring under the old building, which had to collapse. They are the scavengers, the gravediggers, who are expected to remove the semi-ruined old regime, but they are not going to build a new citadel – that will need creative persons, constructive abilities, not people trained in circumventing, in pettifogging, in writing pamphlets under conditions of censorship in which you say one thing and mean another, not sly, cunning, ultimately small-minded lawyers with minds not attuned to the big constructive task of the future. But since the lawyers were the only people the lower classes trusted, because it was they who wrote the revolutionary pamphlets and put them in power, the revolution was lost. The revolution ought to have been conducted by the people who really were the new men, by the great new merchants, the great new captains of industry, the great new bankers, the people who belonged to the modern world.

Here one of Saint-Simon's most original, penetrating and creative ideas comes in. In every age there is a distribution of power. There are the people who matter and the people who do not. There are the people who represent what is coming, the new, and the people who represent what is dying away, the old. In the Middle Ages feudal lords represented the principle of progress because they defended the peasants, who were then the producers of the goods that were needed by humanity. They protected them against interruption of their work, and in general did their best to enhance that particular order. Soldiers were needed by the order too, and priests. Christianity in its day was an immense progressive force, and so long as it was a progressive force the priests who taught it were progressive men, people who taught something more adjusted to the needs of their time than the Roman religion or the Greek religion or the Jewish religion would have been. But they became obsolete, they have given way to quite a different set of men. Today it is not priests, it is not soldiers, it is not feudal lords who matter, it is quite a different class of men: scientists, industrialists, bankers, experts – people, ultimately, who represent science and industry. Science and industry have come to stay, but the only way in which we can organise a world in which human beings can satisfy their wishes is by applying science in the most productive manner, that is to say in the manner that will develop the great new disciplines which are at last rising in the world – commerce, industry, and above all credit banking.

Saint-Simon is very extraordinarily obsessed by the importance of bankers, because he is so committed to the game of
playing historical analogies, so deeply affected by the notion of
history, by the notion of development and evolution, by the fact
that nothing stands still and that everything in one age may
correspond to something (which is never identical) in any other
age. He often asks who corresponds in his own age to the people
who were responsible for unity and centralisation in the Middle
Ages, say, or in the Roman Empire. The Romans were great
because they reigned over almost all mankind and their laws
were universal. The Middle Ages were great because the Church
disciplined the whole world, civilised it, and therefore prevented
strife, prevented provincialism, prevented the waste which is for
Saint-Simon the worst of all crimes – the flooding away, the
complete destruction of human resources in isolated, private,
individual directions. Who is like that now? Banks, he says:
credit is the great octopus, the great universal force which holds
everybody together, and people who slight it, people who defy
it, people who think they can do without it are destroyed by it.
The greatest power in the world is the interconnection of
international finance. But far from attacking it, far from being
against it as an oppressive system which sucks the blood out of
the people (as for example Cobbett or even Sismondi were apt to
do at about that time), he welcomed it as a great riveting,
centralising, connecting force, because unity to him is everything.

The only way in which humanity can develop is by the
rational concentration of its resources, so that every single object
which is possessed, every single art, every single gift, every single
aspiration which people have, shall not be wasted but used in the
best way, directed to its best possible use. Anything which
unifies is better than anything which disintegrates. It is bad
enough to have to obey stupid rulers, but chaos is worse still,
and Saint-Simon, like Hobbes after the English revolution in the
seventeenth century, is frightened above all of meaningless
bloodshed, violence, mobs sweeping through the streets, mad-
dened Jacobins, their heads filled with empty slogans provided
by rhetorical lawyers who do not understand the time in which

they live – hence his worship of industrialists, bankers, men of business, and his conception of society as an enormous business establishment, something like ICI or General Motors. The State for him is already obsolescent, though needed at one time for the protection of individuals against the power of the encroaching Church. Then he suddenly observes that of course the clergy purported to be scientists; but now that the clergy have been discredited there is no further need for protection against them, and therefore the useful, the creative part of the State, which made possible economic and social and spiritual development for human beings without the dead hand of the no longer living Church, is gone, and the State itself has become dead, oppressive and unnecessary. Therefore (he says very firmly) what we need is simply a State which has become a kind of industrial enterprise of which we are all members, a kind of enormous limited liability company – or unlimited liability, perhaps, precisely as envisaged by Burke, who was also historically minded. Saint-Simon demands not merely what Burke calls 'a partnership in all science; a partnership in all art; a partnership in every virtue', although he believes in that, of course, passionately, but also a partnership in the most literal sense (in the sense in which Burke's State was decidedly not meant as a partnership), a partnership in trade, in calico – exactly what Burke denied – a partnership in commerce, in industry, in the sale of all that humans need, and in knowledge, without which men cannot get anything done at all.

What are the purposes of society? Well, says Saint-Simon, we are told it is the common good, but that is very vague. The purpose of society is self-development, the purpose of society is 'the best application, in order to satisfy human needs, of knowledge acquired by the sciences, in the arts and crafts, the dissemination of such knowledge, and the development and maximum accumulation of its fruits, that is, in the most useful combination of all separate activities, in the sphere of the sciences, the arts and crafts'. Enough homage to Alexanders, he says: long live the Archimedeses. Enough homage, in other words, to soldiers, priests and kings. These persons are as dead and obsolete as astrologers and athletes. What we need are scientists and industrialists, because theirs is the realm where the knowledge and the needs of today are to be found. These are the people who get things done. These are the people under whose regime we do in fact live, although we do not know it and they do not know it. They themselves stupidly obey feudal relics, which they do not realise they could flick off with their little finger. But why should we suffer this to happen? The whole of history is the tale of the sordid exploitation of human beings by human beings, which is a most dreadful waste. Why should human beings waste their energies on exploiting other human beings, when they might be exploiting nature? When one human being oppresses another, too much energy is lost, both by the oppressor and by the oppressed, who resists. Let the oppressor cease to oppress; let the resister cease to resist; let them both throw themselves into the sacred task of exploiting the wealth of mankind – nature – building, creating, making a material culture. Hence all those paeans of Saint-Simon's to production, to organisation.

As for rights, 'right' is an empty sound: there are only interests. Interests are that which humanity happens to want at any given moment. It is the business of producers to give it to them. Humanity divides into two vast classes, the idle and the industrious, the *oisifs* and the *producteurs*, he calls them sometimes – the indolent and the workers. By 'workers' he does not seem to mean manual workers or the proletariat; he means anybody who works, including managers, captains of industry, bankers, industrialists.

Above all, we must have professionals and not amateurs. Poverty is always due to incompetence, and we must replace the appalling waste of competition by concerted planning: what we want is a centralised industrial plan for society. We want association in place of competition, we want labour, which must be compulsory if necessary, because that is the end of man, and we want to take every opportunity for the maximum advance of research – and of the arts too, because unless the human imagination is kindled, by artists, by people who work upon the emotions, nothing will occur at all. The arts have their part to play also in this vast human advance, which will consist of the harnessing and conditioning of human emotions, human passions, human energies, towards that which the present age makes so attainable, namely a kind of vast self-effecting industrial system in which everybody will have enough, nobody will be miserable, and all human ills will disappear. In order to conduct the system, we must have élites, because the people have certainly been too busy to create it – here he talks like an eighteenth-century Encyclopaedist – and to run it themselves.

Of whom shall these élites consist? Saint-Simon's view changed through his long life. First he thinks it ought to be scientists, then he alters his view and thinks it ought to be bankers and industrialists. In early life he has mysterious bodies called the Councils of Newton – these are a kind of international co-operative or scientific academy, administered by public subscription and a mysterious system of voting, in which artists and industrialists and mathematicians combine in some inscrutable manner. By the end he has a parliament consisting of three parts. First of all there is the Chamber of Invention, which is populated by engineers and artists – painters, poets and so forth – men who produce, men with ideas, men who, whether in the arts or the sciences, are the first to have flashes of genius. The second chamber sifts and checks: it consists of mathematicians, physicists, physiologists and the like. The final chamber consists of executives – industrialists, bankers, people who really know how to get things done because they understand the nature of the time in which they live and because the sheer struggle for survival, the sheer necessity of competition, has taught them what can be done, and what cannot.

He has various other plans which always come to the same thing – we must produce. We must produce, we must invent. Creativity is the great cry. Every man must realise himself in as many directions as possible. That great medieval notion according to which the flesh was martyred and the human ideal consisted in some kind of self-subjugation, in some kind of self-refusal, in escaping to some inner life from temptations of the flesh and the devils of the outer world – let that be buried for ever. The Christian doctrine that rewards shall be laid up for us in another world, while here the flesh is subordinate to the spirit, must be abolished; harmony between the flesh and the spirit must be introduced. The spirit cannot work without a great material development; no material development can occur without a great spiritual awakening, without the ideas of genius after genius, without general human advance in all possible directions. It is a picture rather like Tintoretto's notion of Paradise – a vast happy conglomeration of humanity holding hands, circling in an endless dance of gaiety and joy in which all their faculties, all their desires, all their inclinations are richly – over-richly – satisfied in the great cornucopias which only the industrialists and the bankers, now no longer oppressed by ancient institutions and ludicrous laws which hem them in, can produce.

About the élite he sounds a very modern note, when he says that they must practise two moralities. What was so wonderful about the priests of Egypt, for example, who were a very early and original élite, was that they believed one thing and fed the population with another. That is good, that is exactly how things should be conducted, because the people cannot be expected to face the truth at once, but must be gradually educated. Consequently we must have a small body of industrialists and bankers and artists who gradually wean mankind, who gradually condition them to take their proper part in the industrial order. That is a familiar kind of neo-feudalism. The great phrase, indeed, on which Communism is built – 'From everyone according to his capacity ...' – comes from Saint-Simon and the Saint-Simonians. Again, when Stalin said that artists – novelists, for example – are 'engineers of human souls', that their business is applied, not pure, that the end of art is not itself, but the moulding and the conditioning of human beings – that is a Saint-Simonian idea. Everybody, then, must be an engineer, whether of unanimated stuff or of human souls. But if this is to be done we cannot have a lot of outworn unintelligible metaphysical beliefs obstructing us. Therefore Saint-Simon devised anti-democracy, for example, because nothing could be achieved by democracy; no great plan can be achieved except by intelligent men who understand the time in which they live, who have power concentrated in their hands and who do things as experts, because only experts can get things done. Only experts

ever have got anything done, and experts will never be overthrown, as by the French Revolution, whose result was bloodshed, chaos and terrible human retrogression.

Similarly, liberty is a ludicrous slogan. Liberty is always
disorganising; liberty is always something negative, against
oppression from outside. But in an advanced regime where
everything is progressive there is no oppression, there is nothing
to resist, there is no need to use a battering ram. Liberty is
always a kind of dynamite which will blow things up, but in a
constructive era, in a creative era as against a destructive one,
dynamite is not to be used – not for that kind of purpose at any
rate. Hence all his cries that individual liberty is dangerous and
must be suppressed.

He deals similarly with *laissez-faire*. At one period he believed
in *laissez-faire*, being a disciple of the man whom he calls 'the
divine Smith'; but *laissez-faire*, again, leads to absolute chaos; it
is quite impossible to get anything done unless we plan things,
direct things from the centre. Consequently we have the terrifying notion of the great neo-feudal hierarchy, with bankers at the
top, industrialists somewhat below them, engineers and techni-
cians below them, then artists and painters and writers. Every
imaginative human being who has something to offer is somewhere in this hierarchy, this great new feudal regime in which
everything is arranged in a rigid order. This is the way in which
advance can be achieved, this is the way in which an army
marches, and we are an army, the whole of history is an army,
for Saint-Simon – he more or less calls it that.

Similarly, he is violently against equality, which he regards as
an idiotic cry on the part of the oppressed masses which should
have nothing to do with a world ordered by rational government. We must have the administration, not of persons, but of
things. The administration of things means leading us towards a
proper goal, which is the satisfaction of wishes by the best –
most efficient – methods possible. If that is to be the human
goal, then the great cry is not equality, not liberty, but fraternity
– for all men certainly are brothers.

This brings us to the last phase of Saint-Simon's thought, his
nouveau christianisme – his new Christianity. He felt towards

the end of his life that a cult was needed, that something must be done, because we do not know by technology alone; that the beliefs of men must be fixed upon something. He says: Consider the age of Cicero; the Romans' religion was dying, although the temples were still visited, and Cicero believed in preserving the outer husk of the Roman religion although he himself no longer believed in its inner essence. This cannot be done. There are plenty of people now who do not believe in the God of Christianity or in Christ or in any of the *dogmata* but who have a good deal of use for the Church because they think it curbs the evil instincts of men. But it is no use when the belief is worn away, the Church will collapse. The shell cannot continue without the yolk. We must therefore create a new religion, a new faith which will respond to the needs of the time. The golden age is before us: it is a blind tradition which places it behind us; we are marching towards it with rapid step. Our children will arrive there; it is for us, he says, to trace the path.

How are we to trace the path? He is not very clear about that. Above all, by association and by love. If human beings understand each others' needs, identify themselves with them, then their creative imaginations will pour themselves out in the direction of the greatest and most harmonious production of those goods which will go to everyone according to his need. Enfantin, the leader of Saint-Simon's sect after he died, said: 'You are an aspect of me, and I am an aspect of you.' Indeed when the sect – for it became a religious sect – went to live in the outskirts of Paris, a special tunic was designed which could only be buckled on from behind, so that every member of the little Saint-Simonian sect was dependent upon someone else. This was a symbol of co-operation rather than competition, and there is an exquisite picture by Raymond Bonheur of the composer Félicien David wearing one of these Saint-Simonian tunics with a great 'D' embroidered in front, incorporating strings like those of a harp. Saint-Simonians were in love with medieval pageantry, and wanted to reconstitute the medieval hierarchy in industrial terms: this is really what is original in Saint-Simonism.

It is quite clear in what way Saint-Simonism influences us whenever there is an attempt to construct a coherent society by applying science to the solution of human problems – not as in the eighteenth century, when it is a question of the solution of perennial problems which are always the same, and in terms of principles which are always the same, which never alter, because they are engraved in the human heart, or because they are discovered in nature or by metaphysical insight or by whatever means; but in terms of values which themselves evolve with the times. We ask which invention affects which other invention, which human beings affect which other human beings, and the notion that one must make human society coherent, that one must create some kind of planned single entity out of it, and not allow human beings to free-wheel, not allow them to do what they want to do simply because they want to do it, because this might interfere with a state of affairs in which many more of their faculties might be realised, if only they knew – that is the Saint-Simonian idea. It takes mild and humane forms in the case of, for example, the American New Deal, or the post-war socialist State in England. It takes violent, ruthless, brutal, fanatical forms in the case of directively planned Fascist and Communist societies. In their case the notion of a new secular religion which should be an opiate for the masses, urging them on towards an idea which they may not intellectually be able to understand, has been taken over from Saint-Simon also. So too has the conflation of the notion that we are part of the historical stream going forward – and therefore there are no absolute ideals, and any ideal is to be estimated in terms of its own perfection, the degree to which it satisfies present needs, not the needs of some past or future age – with the notion that history is a history of altering technology, because technology represents the human spirit at its most active, and humanity is to be divided into those who work and those who do nothing, the drones and the producers, the active and the passive, the doers and the done-to.

At the heart of the whole conception is science, or scientism – the belief that unless things are done under a rigorous discipline by people who alone understand the material of which the world is composed, human and non-human, chaos and frustration are the result. This can only be achieved by the élite. The élite cannot but practise a double morality – one for themselves, one for others. Liberty, democracy, *laissez-faire* individualism, feudalism – all these metaphysical notions, slogans, words which do not mean very much, must go in order to make room for something clearer, bolder, newer: big business, State capitalism, scientific organisation, an organisation of world peace, a world parliament, a world federation. All this is Saint-Simonian.

Saint-Simon did not believe in revolutions, because he had seen one. He believed in powers of persuasion. But revolution need not be the means. The one thing that he cared about most deeply was that humanity itself should at last obtain the satisfaction of its wishes. On his death-bed he said to his disciples, 'There is one thing I wish to say to you: love each other and help one another. My whole life can be summed up in one single thought – to assure all men the freest development of their faculties.' And 'The party of the workers shall be built [by "workers" he meant those who were productive] – the future is with us.' It was, but perhaps not quite in the sense in which Saint-Simon, who was the most liberal, generous, optimistic and ultimately naïve man, believed.

In all this talk about fraternity and love and association and organisation with which the dying Saint-Simon adjures his friends and humanity in general, what about liberty? What about liberty, not perhaps in the empty sense in which he says the eighteenth-century lawyers used it, as a battering-ram against the survival of feudalism, but real liberty, civil liberty, the liberty of human beings to do what they wish within a limited sphere? On this point Saint-Simon says something which strikes a chillier note than anything else he said, for he really was against it. He did not care who put forward his ideas, or how oppressively they were put forward, whether by Napoleon or the Holy Alliance or King Louis XVIII, to all of whom he appeals indifferently. He says that the discussions about liberty which so greatly agitate the middle classes have become a matter of indifference to the lower classes, since we know all too well that in the current state of civilisation the arbitrary use of power does not affect them very much. The small men, the lower classes, the largest and poorest class of mankind, without which no reconstruction of humanity can occur – these people do not care about liberty; they are bored by justice, as the Russian left-wing socialist thinker Chernyshevsky was to say later in the century. What the people want is not parliament, liberty and rights. These are the cravings of the bourgeoisie. What they want is boots, and this cry for bread, boots and not a lot of liberty and liberal slogans then becomes the staple refrain of all the hard-boiled left-wing parties up to Lenin and Stalin. This somewhat sinister note may also be traced to the gentle, humanitarian, noble Saint-Simon.

MAISTRE

Joseph de Maistre was a very frightening figure to many of his contemporaries – frightening because of what he wrote rather than because of what he was. Indeed his contemporaries had not very much chance of meeting him, since the most important years of his life were spent in the service of the King of Sardinia, and at the court of St Petersburg, to which he was appointed as diplomatic representative. He was frightening to them because of the violence, the intransigence and the extremely uncompromising and hard-headed dogmatism with which he wished to strike down the doctrines of which he disapproved.

The normal view of him is fairly stated by Émile Faguet, perhaps the most accurate and the fairest-minded critic of Maistre in France in the nineteenth century. He calls Maistre 'a fierce absolutist, a furious theocrat, an intransigent legitimist, apostle of a monstrous trinity composed of Pope, King and Hangman, always and everywhere the champion of the hardest, narrowest and most inflexible dogmatism, a dark figure out of the Middle Ages, part learned doctor, part inquisitor, part executioner'. And again, 'his Christianity is terror, passive obedience and the religion of the State'; his faith is merely 'a slightly touched-up paganism'; he is a 'Praetorian of the Vatican'. An admirer speaks of his 'Christianity of terror'; Edgar Quinet, a Protestant under the influence of the German romantics, writes of Maistre's 'inexorable God aided by the hangman; the Christ of a permanent Committee of Public Safety'; and in our own day the Spanish philosopher Miguel de Unamuno refers to Maistre's 'slaughter-house'.

This is the usual portrait of him, largely invented by Sainte-Beuve, and perpetuated by various other thinkers in the nineteenth century. Maistre is painted, always, as a fanatical monarchist and a still more fanatical supporter of papal authority; proud, bigoted, inflexible, with a strong will and an unbelievable power of rigid reasoning from dogmatic premises to extreme and unpalatable conclusions; brilliant, embittered, a medieval doctor born out of his time, vainly seeking to arrest the current of history; a distinguished anomaly, formidable, hostile, solitary and ultimately pathetic; at best a tragic patrician figure, defying and denouncing a shifty and vulgar world, into which he had been incongruously born; at worst an unbending, self-blinded die-hard pouring curses upon the marvellous new age whose benefits he was too wilful to see, and too callous to feel.

His works are regarded as interesting and *outré* rather than important – the last despairing effort of feudalism in the dark ages to resist the march of progress. He is described either as a brave but doomed paladin of a lost cause, or as a foolish or odious survival of the older and more heartless generation, according to whatever attitude the nineteenth-century critics happen to take. But both sides, whether for or against him, always assume that his day is done, that his world has no relevance to anything contemporary. This is the point of view which is shared alike by Victor Hugo and Lamennais, by Sainte-Beuve and Faguet, by James Stephen and Morley, and particularly by Harold Laski, who wrote an essay on him in which he took the view that Maistre was to be rejected as a played-out force.

This view, which may have been intelligible in the nineteenth century, seems absurd in the present age. For although Maistre may have spoken the language of the past, the content of what he had to say is the absolute substance of anti-democratic talk of our day; in comparison with his progressive contemporaries he is really ultra-modern, born not so much after as before his time. If his ideas did not have more immediate influence, it is because the soil in his own time was unreceptive. His doctrines, and still more his attitude of mind, had to wait a century before they came – as come they did – into their own.

Maistre's task, in his own eyes, was to destroy everything which the eighteenth century had built up. Let me explain how he came by this state of mind. He was born in 1753 in Chambéry in Savoy, then part of the Kingdom of Piedmont-Sardinia. This Kingdom, of which Maistre was a subject all his life, was relatively enlightened in the eighteenth century: it abolished feudalism a good many years before the French did so. Like other liberal aristocrats, Maistre was a mild reformer, not particularly reactionary and not particularly bigoted. He was a grown man when the Revolution finally broke out. He was over thirty, and like others who went through the Revolution – like Saint-Simon, like Schiller, like Hegel – he took most violently against it. The spectacle of the Jacobin Terror was something which he never forgot for the rest of his life, and this is what turned him into an implacable enemy of everything that is liberal, democratic, high-minded, everything connected with intellectuals, critics, scientists, everything which was to do with the kind of forces which created the French Revolution. When he talks about Voltaire he talks about him almost as if he were a personal enemy.

Being a Savoyard, Maistre entered the royal service, and began writing pamphlets, after the French revolutionaries had invaded Savoy, against the Revolution. These pamphlets were very sharp: they had a peculiar freshness, indeed a ferocity, which immediately attracted attention. But the King of Sardinia felt that he was an uncomfortable man to have about the court. The court was very small, very limited, rather provincial, and Maistre was too brilliant, too active, too imaginative and too interesting a man to be altogether comfortable there. But he was obviously very able, and he attracted a great deal of attention by the brilliance of his writings. Consequently it was decided to send him as far away as possible, and he was duly sent away to St Petersburg as a minister of the King of Sardinia, or the equivalent of a minister, from 1803 until he left in 1817.

In St Petersburg he was regarded as a man of particular charm, courtesy, urbanity; he was a brilliant and agreeable conversationalist, delightful company and greatly sought after in society. He enjoyed his life in St Petersburg; he was fascinated by the

Russian monarchy, and he got on very well with the immediate circles around Alexander I; indeed, that Emperor used him as a political adviser at various moments during his reign.

After the war against Napoleon was over, for some reason Alexander demanded his recall; it may be that he had converted too many ladies of fashion to the Roman Church. Several of these ladies were destined to play a very large part in Catholic circles in Western Europe. Possibly he interfered a little too much in Russian policy, with so strong a personality; at any rate, the King of Sardinia, now restored to his throne, was induced to recall him. Maistre went back to Turin, the capital, was given a sinecure, and died, in considerable honour but with no kind of political power, or indeed any other kind of power, in 1821. His reputation is largely posthumous.

The aim to which Maistre addressed himself most vigorously, as I say, was to destroy the eighteenth century, and the thought of the eighteenth century. It is a mistake to assume that the thought of the eighteenth century was a seamless garment; indeed, some of the eighteenth-century thinkers were divided by deep differences. But there are certain things which are common to them all. They might not all believe in progress; they might not all believe in God; they might not all believe in the immortality of the soul. Some of them believed in intuition; others believed in empiricism. Some believed in spontaneity and simplicity of feeling; others believed in science and sophistication. What they had in common was the belief that men were by nature, if not good, at any rate not bad, potentially benevolent, and that each man was the best expert on his own interests and his own values, when he was not being bamboozled by knaves or fools; that on the whole men were prone to follow the rules of conduct which their own understanding provided. Most thinkers of the eighteenth century believed that progress was desirable – that is to say, for example, that freedom was better than slavery; that legislation founded on what was called 'the precepts of nature' could right almost every wrong; that nature was only reason in action, and its workings, therefore, could in principle be deduced from a set of axioms like those of a theory in geometry, or like those of physics and chemistry, if only you knew them. They believed that all things that were good and true and virtuous and free were necessarily compatible, and indeed more than that, that they were interconnected. The more empirically-minded among them were sure that the science of human nature could be developed no less than that of inanimate things, that ethical and political questions, provided they were genuine – and how could they not be so? – could be answered no less certainly than those of mathematics and astronomy, and that a life founded upon these answers would be free, secure, happy and wise. They believed that the millennium could be reached by the use of faculties and the practice of methods which had for over a century, in the spheres both of knowledge and of action, led to triumphs more magnificent than any hitherto attained in human history. That, roughly speaking, is the common belief, the general temper and attitude, of the rational thinkers of the eighteenth century.

All this Maistre set himself to destroy completely. Any characteristic of the eighteenth century of this kind he was determined to root up so that it should stand no more. He took on this enormous task because he believed that the Revolution in which the innocent had suffered was an appalling disaster. He had loved and admired France from outside (he was on the margins of it in Savoy) with the peculiar passion which people on the edges of countries have for those countries when they wish to be identified with them – there are many instances of this in history. With the peculiar indignation born of the desire to demolish a really golden ideal, he determined to discredit the forces which in his opinion were responsible for the destruction of his dream. Therefore, in place of the a priori formulae of this idealistic sociology, he decided to appeal to the empirical facts of history and to observe human behaviour. In place of the ideals of progress, liberty, perfectibility he preached the sacredness of the past, the virtue, and the necessity, indeed, of complete subjection, because of the incurably bad and corrupt nature of man. In place of science he preached the primacy of instinct, superstition, prejudice. In place of optimism, pessimism. In place of eternal harmony and eternal peace, the necessity – for him the divine necessity – of conflict, of suffering, of bloodshed, of war.

In the place of peace and social equality, of common interests and the simple nature of the uncorrupted natural man about whom Rousseau had talked, he insisted that what was important was diversity, inequality, conflict of interests – those were the normal conditions of individuals and of nations. He denied all meaning to such abstractions as Nature, Man, Natural Rights. His doctrine of language contradicted everything which Condorcet and Condillac and all the great scientists of the eighteenth century had tried to formulate. He tried to breathe new life into the discredited doctrine of the Divine Right of Kings. He defended the importance of mystery, of darkness, almost of ignorance, and above all of irrationality, as the basis of social and political life. With immense effectiveness and brilliance he denounced every form of lucidity, every form of rationality. Temperamentally Maistre was as ruthless and as extreme as his great enemies, the Jacobins; and he had something of their faith and their integrity.

Alexander Herzen, the Russian revolutionary, remarks that what distinguished the men of 1792 was the wonderful completeness of their rejection of the entire old order. He says that they denounced not merely its vices, but all its virtues too. They wished to leave nothing standing, they wanted to destroy the entire evil system, root and branch, in order to build up something absolutely fresh, entirely pure. They wanted to make no compromise; they wanted to have no debt to that upon whose ruins their new cities would be raised. Maistre was the exact inverse of this. He attacked eighteenth-century rationalism with the intolerance and the passion and the power and the gusto of the great revolutionaries themselves. He wanted to destroy what has so well been called 'the heavenly city of the eighteenth-century philosophers'. He wanted to raze it to the ground, not leaving stone upon stone.

The method which he used, as well as the truths which he preached, although he officially said he derived them from Thomas à Kempis or Thomas Aquinas, or the great preachers of the seventeenth century in France, Bourdaloue or Bossuet, in fact displays very little of the spirit of these great pillars of the Church. They had far more to do with the anti-rationalist approach of someone like Augustine, or with the Freemasons and the illuminists among whom Maistre's youth was spent.

Maistre's fundamental doctrine is this: nature is red in tooth and claw, it is a vast scene of carnage and destruction. The men of the eighteenth century turn to metaphysics, to logic, even to geometry, in order to find out what nature is like. Those are not the sources of our knowledge of nature. If they want to talk about nature, let them be serious. They speak about using observation as a weapon, using our eyes, not accepting a great many dogmatic truths merely because a lot of preachers have spoken to us about them. Very well then, they must be taken at their word. Let us look at what is going on round us, Maistre says, let us not look at books, let us look at nature, at ourselves, let us study history, yes, and zoology. They are the true guides to nature. What do we see if this is where we look? Let me quote what Maistre says:

> In the vast domain of living nature there reigns an open violence, a kind of prescriptive fury which arms all the creatures to their common doom. As soon as you leave the inanimate kingdom, you find the decree of violent death inscribed on the very frontiers of life. You feel it already in the vegetable kingdom: from the vast catalpa to the humblest herb, how many plants *die*, and how many are *killed*! But from the moment you enter the animal kingdom, this law is suddenly in the most dreadful evidence. A violent power, at once hidden and palpable . . . has in each major subdivision of the animals appointed a certain number of species to devour the others. Thus there are insects of prey, reptiles of prey, birds of prey, fishes of prey, quadrupeds of prey. There is no instant of time when one creature is not being devoured by another. Over all these numerous races of animals man is placed, and his destructive hand spares nothing that lives.

The passage which follows is more effective in French. It is a curious litany:

> il tue pour se nourrir, il tue pour se vêtir, il tue pour se parer, il tue pour attaquer, il tue pour se défendre, il tue pour s'instruire, il tue pour s'amuser, il tue pour tuer: roi superbe et terrible, il a besoin de

tout, et rien ne lui résiste. . . . à l'agneau [il demande] ses entrailles pour faire résonner une harpe . . . au loup sa dent la plus meurtrière pour polir les ouvrages légers de l'art, à l'éléphant ses défenses pour façonner le jouet d'un enfant: ses tables sont couvertes de cadavres . . . Cependant quel être [dans le carnage permanent] exterminera celui qui les extermine tous? Lui. C'est l'homme qui est chargé d'égorger l'homme . . . Ainsi s'accomplit . . . la grande loi de la destruction violente des êtres vivants. La terre entière, continuellement imbibée de sang, n'est qu'un autel immense où tout ce qui vit doit être immolé sans fin, sans mesure, sans relâche, jusqu'à la consommation des choses, jusqu'à l'extinction du mal, jusqu'à la mort de la mort.

Let me translate this:

Man kills to obtain food and kills to clothe himself. He kills to adorn himself and he kills in order to attack. He kills in order to defend himself and he kills in order to instruct himself. He kills to amuse himself and he kills in order to kill. Proud and terrible king, he wants everything and nothing can resist him . . . From the lamb [he demands] its guts to make his harp resound . . . from the wolf his deadliest tooth to polish his trifling works of art, from the elephant his tusks to make a toy for his child: his tables he covers with corpses . . . But who [in the general carnage] will exterminate the one who exterminates all the others? He will himself. It is man who is charged with the slaughter of men . . . Thus is accomplished . . . the great law of the violent destruction of living creatures. The whole earth, perpetually steeped in blood, is nothing but a vast altar, upon which all that is living must be sacrificed without end, without measure, without pause, until the consummation of things, until evil is extinct, until the death of death.

And yet, says Maistre, man is born to love. He is tender and gentle and good. Whence comes his divine fury? Is it the earth calling for blood? Why is it, asks Maistre, that troops in battle never, or very seldom, mutiny against the instructions of their commanders, who tell them to exterminate other innocent men? Is there not something paradoxical in the fact that soldiers – innocent, honourable men, whom we receive with the greatest courtesy in private life, and who in ordinary life are gentle, virtuous, God-fearing, polite persons, who would not hurt a fly – go into battle in order to kill other soldiers, as innocent as themselves, without any demur? Whereas the executioner, who is the man, after all, who, under instruction, kills people who on the whole are presumably not innocent – parricides, murderers and other criminals – and kills many fewer of them than the soldiers do, is nevertheless regarded as a social outcast; nobody shakes him by the hand; he is regarded with horror and loathing, not as an ordinary member of society. Is there not something strange in admiring the shedding of innocent blood, and recoiling before the shedding of guilty blood? It must be, says Maistre, because war is in some sense divine in itself, because it is the law of the world. This is a central doctrine in Maistre: that rationalist notions do not work. If you really want to know why people behave as they do, you must seek the answer in the realm of the irrational. This is a mysticism which puts its faith in the other world, not in this one.

Maistre is fascinated by the spectacle of war. Consider, he says, a battlefield. People imagine that a battlefield is a place where things happen in a planned manner. The commander gives orders, the troops march into battle, and battles are won or lost in accordance with the preponderance of troops, or the skilful instructions issued by the generals. Nothing could be less true. Consider an actual battle. Once more, do not look at the textbook, look at life: zoology and history are Maistre's masters. If you find a battlefield, what you will encounter upon it is not at all an orderly procession of events matching the descriptions of eye-witnesses, or even of strategists, of tacticians or historians. What you will find is appalling noise, confusion, slaughter, death, ruin, the shrieks of the wounded, the groans of the dying, the violent firing of firearms. 'Five or six kinds of intoxication' possess people upon the field; a general cannot possibly tell whether he is losing the battle or winning it. Nobody can possibly tell this. Wars are not won by rational calculation, they are won by moral force. They are won by people who feel they are winning them. They are won by some kind of irrational inner certainty. You cannot, in the moment of battle, calculate whether your troops are still more numerous upon the field of battle than the enemy's. It is not like a duel between two human beings, where the strength of one is obviously greater or obviously smaller than the strength of the other. Battles are won psychologically, battles are won by acts of faith. What happens happens as a result of some kind of mysterious inner force which is certainly not rational calculation or the careful application of a textbook set of rules, some kind of elaborate rational calculation or plan which wins or loses battles.

Tolstoy, when describing the Battle of Borodino in *War and Peace*, carefully followed this account of Maistre's. Tolstoy read Maistre because Maistre lived in Petersburg during the period in which he was interested, and he echoes his description of what a real battle is like, describing the experience of people present at the battle rather than giving the orderly, tidied-up account constructed later by eye-witnesses or historians. For both Maistre and Tolstoy, too, life itself is a battle of this sort, and any attempt to describe it in rational terms is a dreadful distortion, a smoothing over, tidying up, ordering of something which is by nature deeply irrational, deeply untidy, and obeys no discoverable laws or rules.

Maistre protests above all against the assumption that reason is the great mistress of things. It is impossible to govern men or achieve anything by means of reason. He says: What do you think reason is to me? Reason is simply a feeble faculty in men for the purpose, now and then, of fitting means to ends. You really think that the great institutions of mankind are rational constructions? Remember that the business of an institution is to be authoritative. The business of government is to govern. Every human society must have a government, and every government must have this sovereignty. Every sovereignty must contain within it a principle of infallibility, and the only thing that is absolutely infallible is the word of God. Anything which human beings make, human beings can mar. Anything which human beings can construct, human beings can destroy. Suppose you create an artificial institution, a republic or a limited constitutional monarchy, by means of that reason which the eighteenth century recommended – say some utilitarian arrangement for the securing of the greatest happiness or the greatest freedom of the greatest number. Well, clever men construct that in one generation, and still cleverer men in the next generation can puncture it full of holes, can completely destroy it by means of their superior, their still subtler, still cleverer, still more destructive reasoning. Nothing can stand perpetually but what something other than reason builds up, for what reason builds up, reason will pull down.

Man is by nature vicious, wicked, cowardly and bad. What the Roman Church says, what Christianity says, about original guilt, original sin, is the truest psychological insight into human nature. Left alone, human beings will tear each other to pieces. Here Maistre is completely opposed to his time: he regards human beings, unless clamped with iron rings and held down by means of the most rigid discipline, as likely to destroy themselves. He regards human nature as fundamentally self-annihilating, and needing to be curbed and controlled. The only thing which is reliable, the only thing which is dependable, is not man-made; for if it is man-made it can equally be unmade by man.

What did the eighteenth century teach us about this? It taught us that society was founded upon a contract. But this is a logical as well as a historical absurdity. What is a contract? A contract is a promise. So we have a lot of rational persons coming together – says Maistre in a mocking manner – for the purpose of arranging a peaceful life which will give people rather more of worldly goods, or security, or happiness, or liberty, or whatever it is they may happen to want, than they would get in a so-called state of nature. And how do they do this? By constructing a State as one might a bank, or a limited-liability company. But even to do that requires that the promise, the social contract, be enforceable. If somebody breaks it there must be some kind of instrument for the purpose of forcing him back into conformity, or expelling him. But a body of men who already understand such concepts as promises, and the enforcement of promises, is a completely mature, sophisticated human society. The notion that barbarous creatures, wild aborigines from the woods, coming together for the first time in history in order to construct something called a social contract, are already furnished with such elaborate and sophisticated social notions as promises towards each other, obligation, duty, enforcement of promises, that they have all this ready to put into the intellectual pool, is a grotesque logical absurdity. People who are armed with the notion of a promise, the notion of respecting each other's will, the notion of punishment, the notion of reward, do not need a society, they are in it already. Quite clearly, therefore, society is presupposed by the notion of a contract. Furthermore, it was not created by man, for if it had been created by man it would not have stood up to the ravages of centuries. It lies in the deep darkness of antiquity; and for Maistre (here he is deeply influenced by Burke) anything which goes back to the mists of antiquity was made by God and not by man.

Similarly with language. M. Rousseau, he says, tells us that he wants to know about the origins of language. Well, of course M. Condillac, who can answer all questions, can answer this question too. How was language constructed? Why, of course, by the division of labour. A lot of rationalist persons, seeking their own personal advantage, cosily gathered together and proceeded to invent language, says Maistre. The first generation of men, presumably, said BA and the next generation of men said BE. The Assyrians invented the nominative, and the Medes invented the genitive. That is how grammar was made.

This kind of bitter irony is very appropriate. Maistre was one of the first to perceive that the whole eighteenth-century notion that human institutions are constructed by rational men for limited and intelligible purposes is totally untrue to human nature. Herder had had some such ideas already, and of course the German romantics had them too. Maistre employed a particularly biting and mordant irony for the purpose of dismantling the rickety structures of eighteenth-century theories about the origins of society, especially their peculiarly unhistorical approach. But his most savage onslaughts are directed against the notion of nature. M. Rousseau, he says, tells us that it is strange that man, who was born free, should be everywhere in chains: 'What does he mean? . . . This mad pronouncement, *Man is born free*, is the opposite of the truth.' Faguet encapsulates

Maistre's response to Rousseau in a brilliant epigram: Rousseau's claim, he says, is as if one were to say how strange it is that sheep, who were born carnivorous, should nevertheless everywhere be nibbling grass. Maistre mocks at the all-providing, all-explaining entity which is dignified by the name of Nature by the Encyclopaedists. Who is this lady, he says, of whom one hears so much? Nature, so far from being the beneficent provider of all good things, the source of all life and knowledge and happiness, is to him an eternal mystery; savage in her methods, the principal source of cruelty, pain, chaos; no doubt serving God's inscrutable purpose, but seldom the source of comfort or enlightenment.

Rousseau had preached a return to the simple virtues of the noble savage. What noble savage? Savages are, according to Maistre, not noble at all but sub-human, cruel, dissident and brutal. Anyone who has lived among them can testify that they are the refuse of mankind. So far from being the great uncorrupted prototypes, early exemplars of natural taste and natural morality, virtuous, high-minded, truthful, from which civilisation has perverted the nations of the West, they are merely the failures of God's creative process. It is true that Christian missionaries who have been sent among the Indians of America, for example, speak about them with kindness, but that is because they are good priests who cannot bring themselves to attribute to any of God's creatures the squalor and the vices in which all these people were in fact sunk. It does not follow from their testimony that the Indians are models for us to follow. The language of savages is not something with primitive strength, with the beauty of a beginning; it has only the confusion and the ugliness of decay.

As for the state of nature, which – for the thinkers of the eighteenth century – acts as a repository of the so-called rights of man which primitive man is supposed to be recognising, in whose name do these eighteenth-century speakers affect to speak? In the name of nature? There is no such lady, says Maistre, otherwise why have we never met her? What are these rights? Inherent in what men? No metaphysical magic eye will detect abstract entities called rights, not derived from either human or divine authority. As for the famous abstract Man in whose name the great revolution was started, in whose name the cruellest massacres were organised, in the name of whom innocents were slaughtered: 'In the course of my life,' says Maistre, 'I have seen Frenchmen, Italians, Russians ... I know, too, thanks to Montesquieu, *that one can be a Persian*. But as for man, I declare that I have never met him in my life; if he exists, he is unknown to me.'

In our day, says Maistre, what has happened as a result of faith in completely empty words and empty formulae is that 'the two anchors of society – religion and slavery – having failed at one and the same moment, the ship was carried away by the storm, and was wrecked'. That is why, in his advice to the Russian Emperor, he was always saying: There are only two anchors upon which society rests, by which wicked man can be confined, protected from his blindly self-destructive impulses. One is the Church and the other is slavery. The Christian Church abolished slavery because it was powerful enough to keep man in fetters by herself, but if you in Russia, where the Orthodox Church is not very highly regarded by the populace, let serfdom go, if you, as your advisers tell you, liberate the serfs, why then your country will be plunged into the most vicious revolution. It will go from barbarism into anarchy. Nobody can want as violently as the Russians want, and once you allow all these 'Pugachevs of the University', as he calls them, all these intellectual rebels, all these economists and scientists and sophisters and magicians, to dominate you, then your kingdom – which rests upon authority as all kingdoms must rest, upon faith in blind authority – will collapse.

What is the principal notion of the eighteenth century? That society is founded upon recognition of reciprocal interests by people who want to live together as happily and as freely as possible. This is denied forcefully and passionately by Maistre. He says society is not founded upon this at all. Society is founded upon self-immolation. Why do soldiers march to battle? They do not know. If a king wishes to introduce something as harmless as a census or the alteration of a calendar, there are mutinies and riots among the population. But if there is a war, in which many innocent men will be slaughtered, and in which many hundreds of thousands will not come back to their wives and children, then people peacefully obey. Why, we cannot tell; it is irrational.

Maistre really makes two points here. One is that the cause of things cannot be fathomed by the mere feeble contrivance of men; the other, that the only things which last are irrational. For example, he says, take the institution of hereditary monarchy: what could be more irrational? Why should a wise king have an equally wise son, or indeed a son who is wise at all? Here is an institution of a patently idiotic nature, for which no good reason can be given, and yet it lasts. It has lasted for many centuries, and upon it the foundations of the Western world are built. But far more rational, far more logical and reasonable, would be to abolish such a monarchy and see what happens. What happened to the unhereditary, elected monarchy in Poland? There chaos and ruin followed almost immediately. Why? Because a rational system had been adopted. Take the institution of marriage. What could be more irrational than that two human beings, merely because they happen to love each other at one stage of their lives, should be together with each other for the rest of their lives, for no better reason than that this happened in the past? But nothing is more short-lived, nothing more destructive, nothing becomes so hateful as the regime of free love. So he goes on, from institution to institution, paradoxically asserting that whatever is irrational lasts, and that whatever is rational collapses; it collapses because anything which is constructed by reason can be pulverised by reason; anything which was built by the self-critical faculties cannot stand up to attack by them. The only thing which can ever dominate men is impenetrable mystery.

The eighteenth century thinks – and the seventeenth century thought, too – that there are certain social and political questions which can be answered in a certain fashion. Some think they can be answered by metaphysicians, others by scientists; some by the word of conscience, by looking into the heart, and others by reading the books of specific experts on these matters. Maistre says: Once you allow such a question to be put, the answer will demand the next question. The answer will never stand up, and people will question the answer, and the answer to that question in turn, and will go on asking for the why of the why of the why. The only way to get people to live in societies at all is to stop them from questioning, and the only way in which you can stop them from questioning is by terror. Only if the heart of things is dark and mysterious, impenetrable, will people obey. Once they have penetrated the heart of things, and once it is rational, once it is something which they can understand, they will not be afraid of it. They will not be in awe of it, they will not revere it, and so it will collapse. What we need, therefore, is something dark and unintelligible.

Take the problem of language, says Maistre. Language is identical with thought. The eighteenth century, which thought that language was a human invention, was mistaken on this point. In order to invent you have to think, and in order to think you have to employ symbols; to say that language can be constructed is an absolute absurdity. M. Condorcet wants to have a scientific language which will be clear and intelligible, which can be spread among all the nations – a kind of scientific Esperanto. Nothing would be more disastrous. It would be disastrous precisely because it was clear, precisely because it was intelligible. Clarity, intelligibility must be put out of court, must be stopped, because it is they which create unrest, criticism, questioning, which end in the overturning of ancient institutions, in injustice, blood, revolutions and chaos.

Latin is the language which we must teach our children. Why? Because it is unclear. People argue against prejudice, against superstition. What is prejudice? It is merely the beliefs of the centuries, tested by experience. History is, after all, the only teacher we have, and politics is only experimental history. Here Maistre talks rather like Burke, who defended prejudice in exactly the same way. Prejudice is simply the skin which humanity has acquired in the course of centuries, traditionally, which has been tested against many diverse situations, and to throw it away is to remain trembling and naked before the destructive forces of life. Latin is a language of an irregular kind. Latin is a language whose grammar is not rational. It embodies all kinds of prejudices, all kinds of ancient superstitions, blind faith, unconscious experience, everything which science is against. That is why it is the language to which we must cling, for there are only two things which are ever good in the world – one is antiquity, and the other is irrationality. Only the combination of these two creates a force sufficiently powerful to resist the corrosive influence of the critics, the askers of questions, the scientists.

Against whom are we trying to preserve the social order? The enemies of the social order, whom Maistre calls 'la secte', are a very interesting collection of men. They are, for him, Jansenists and Calvinists, and all Protestants in general; lawyers, metaphysicians, journalists, writers, Jews, American revolutionaries, intellectuals, scientists, critics; in short, the intelligentsia, and everything which belongs to it. This list – of liberals, of all kinds of critics, of all kinds of people who believe in some sort of abstract truth, of people who do not accept the dogmatic premises of society – was compiled almost for the first time by Maistre, and by now it is familiar. It has been the stock-in-trade of every violently reactionary, Fascist movement of our day.

But of all these Maistre hates scientists the most. They are the people who have the least capacity for understanding life, and for government, and he warned the Tsar of Russia, in extremely solemn tones, not to commit the fatal blunder of allowing the arts and the sciences to dominate the country. He says: Take the greatest nation that ever was, at any rate the greatest in the art of government, the Romans. They knew very well that they would merely make fools of themselves as scientists. They hired Greeks because they knew they would merely be undignified if they tried to do the job themselves. No great statesman, he says, from Suger to Richelieu, was ever a scientist, or knew anything about science. There is something about science, about its dry, abstract, unconcrete nature, something about the fact that it is divorced from the crooked, the chaotic, the irrational texture of life with all its darkness, which makes scientists incapable of adapting themselves to the actual facts, and anyone who listens to them is automatically doomed. He says to the Emperor of Russia: Do not allow all these Lutheran Germans to come and teach in your schools. Who are these people who are pouring in, in endless numbers, into your kingdom? Good men – family men, men who have traditions, faith, religion, respectable morals – do not leave their countries. Only the feckless and the restless and the critical do so. This is the first real sermon against refugees, against freedom of the spirit, against the circulation of humanity – the first, certainly, made in violent and intelligible and, indeed, memorable terms.

What then does society rest upon? Society is part of the vale of tears where we cannot understand the sources of things, where God governs us in an inscrutable way. It rests upon terror; it rests upon obedience, blind obedience to authority. Without it institutions become chaotic and restless, and go down in a welter of disaster. What represents this element of terror? Here Maistre makes a most paradoxical observation, and writes the most famous page in all his writings. He says that the person who stands in the centre of it all is none other than that hated figure, the executioner. Let me quote the famous passage in which he speaks of him:

Who is this inexplicable being? . . . He is like a world in himself . . . Hardly has he been assigned to his proper dwelling-place . . . when others remove their homes elsewhere . . . In the midst of this desolation . . . he lives alone with his mate and his young, who acquaint him with the sound of the human voice. But for them he would hear nothing but shrieks of agony . . . One of the lowest menials of justice knocks at his door and tells him that his services are wanted. He goes. He arrives in a public square where people are crowded together with faces of expectancy. A prisoner, a parricide, a man who has committed a sacrilege is flung to his feet. He seizes the man, stretches him, ties him to a cross which is lying on the ground, raises his arms, and there is a terrible silence. It is broken only by the sound of the crushing of bones under the blows of the iron mace, and the screams of the victim. He unbinds the man, he carries him to the wheel; the broken limbs are twined round the spokes and the head hangs down; the hair stands on end and from the mouth – open like the door of a glowing furnace – there come at intervals only a few broken syllables of entreaty for death. The executioner has finished his task; his heart is beating, but it is with pleasure; he is satisfied with his work. He says in his heart, 'No man breaks on the wheel better than I.' He comes down from the scaffold and holds out his bloody hand, into which, from a distance, an official flings a few gold pieces. The executioner carries them off between two rows of human beings who shrink from him with horror. He sits down to table and eats, he goes to bed and sleeps, but when he awakes next morning his thoughts run on everything but his occupation of the day before. Is he a man? Yes, God allows him to enter his shrines and accepts his prayers. He is no criminal, and yet no human language dares to calls him, for instance, virtuous, honourable or estimable . . . Nevertheless all greatness, all power, all social order depends upon the executioner; he is the terror of human society and the tie that holds it together. Take away this incomprehensible force from the world, and at that very moment order is superseded by chaos, thrones fall, society disappears. God, who is the source of the power of the ruler, is also the source of punishment. He has suspended our world upon these two poles, 'for the Lord is the lord of the twin poles, and round them he sets the world revolving'.

This is not a mere sadistic meditation about crime and punishment. Lamennais said of Maistre that it is strange how a man who is so noble should have only two realities in his whole life: crime and punishment. 'It is as if all his works were written from the scaffold.' But my quotation from Maistre is not merely cruel. It is the expression of a genuine conviction, coherent with all the rest of Maistre's passionate but very lucid thought, that men can only be saved by being hemmed in by the terror of authority. They must be reminded at every instant of their lives of the frightening mystery that lies at the heart of creation; must be purged by perpetual suffering, must be humbled by being made conscious of their stupidity, malice, helplessness at every turn. War, torture, suffering are the inescapable human lot.

Man is a fool; man is a child; man is a lunatic; man is an absentee landlord; life is – ought to be – a kind of penal settlement with guardians to look after this creature. He must be controlled by appointed masters – people who are imbued with a duty which has been laid upon them by their maker, who made nature a hierarchy – by the ruthless imposition of rules, and the ruthless extermination of the enemy. The enemy, as we have seen, is 'la secte', the disturbers, the subverters, the secular reformers, the intellectuals, the idealists, the lawyers, the perfect-ibilians, the people who believe in conscience, or equality, or the rational organisation of society, the liberators, the revolution-aries – these are the people who must be rooted out.

There is something very extraordinary about a man who, in the most lucid possible manner, speaking a language which is certainly as clear and as beautiful as that used by anybody in the eighteenth century, says things which are the precise opposite of the general tenor of that century. Yet Maistre is also in a sense a child of the century, precisely because of the extraordinary contrariety with which he meets every single thing that the century says. Saint-Simon believed that there was something in common between Maistre and the people whom he most particularly disliked, the followers of Voltaire – indeed, even Voltaire himself. Voltaire was the enemy, and Maistre talks with immense hatred about the perpetual hideous grin of this dread-ful monster. Yet Saint-Simon says that perhaps the future of human society lies in the combination of Maistre and Voltaire.

At first this is a wild paradox. How can there be such a combination? Voltaire stands for individual liberty and Maistre for chains. Voltaire cries for more light and Maistre for more darkness. Voltaire hated the Church so violently he denied it even the minimum of virtue; Maistre liked even its vices and regarded Voltaire as the Devil incarnate. Yet there is something in what Saint-Simon says, very odd as it may seem, because, although they are polar opposites, both Voltaire and Maistre belong to the hard, cold, dry, lucid, tough-minded tradition of French thought. Their ideas may appear strictly to contradict one another, but the quality of mind is often exceedingly similar. Neither is guilty of any degree of softness or vagueness or self-indulgence, nor do they tolerate these qualities in others. They stand for the dry against the moist; they are implacably opposed to everything which is turbid and misty, romantic, gushing, impressionistic. Both of them are equally opposed to the spirit of Rousseau, Chateaubriand, Victor Hugo, Michelet, Renan, Bergson. They are ruthless and deflationary writers; they are heartless and, at times, genuinely cynical. Beside this cold, clear, glossy surface even Stendhal's prose – and Stendhal borrowed a great deal from Maistre – seems romantic. Marx, Tolstoy, Sorel, Lenin – they are their true successors.

This tendency to cast a cold look upon the political scene, to deflate and to dehydrate, to submit politics and history to a genuinely ruthless as opposed to a merely shocking analysis – this is what has entered modern political techniques to a great degree, and it has entered them equally from just such ideas as those of Voltaire and of Maistre. The violently deflationary atmosphere of Voltaire was responsible for the exposure of sentimental popular values. Maistre stresses historicism and political pragmatism, and has a low estimate of the human capacity for goodness, plus a belief that the essence of life is the craving for suffering and sacrifice and surrender. If you add to this Maistre's belief that government is impossible without repression of the weak majority by a minority of dedicated rulers, hardened against all temptation to indulge in any kind of humanitarianism, we are gradually approaching modern totalitarianism. Voltaire can be made to strip away the liberal delusion, Maistre to provide the nostrum by which the bleak, bare world which results can be subdued. True, Voltaire did not like either despotism or deception; and Maistre recognised the need for both. 'The principle of the sovereignty of the people', says Maistre, 'is so dangerous that, even if it were true, it would be necessary to conceal it.' So what Saint-Simon said was not so paradoxical after all. The combination of the two leads to the ruthless totalitarianism, whether of the right or of the left, of the twentieth century.

What really fascinates Maistre is power. Power, for him, is divine. It is the source of all life, of all action. It is the paramount factor in the development of mankind, and whoever knows how to wield it acquires the right to use it; it is by that token the instrument chosen by God, at that particular moment, to work his mysterious purpose. To recognise power where it truly lies – in ancient, established, socially created institutions, not made by the hand of man – is political and moral insight and wisdom. All usurpation must fail in the end, because it flouts the divine laws of the universe. Permanent power, therefore, resides only in him who is the instrument of such laws. To resist power is criminal childishness and folly, directed against the human future.

Maistre preached the doctrine that all events must be studied empirically if we are to understand the workings of the divine will. His stoicism and relativism, his interest in nature and the distribution of power over human beings – these constitute Maistre's deeply considered view, and that is why, strangely, he approved of the Jacobins, which did not make him any more popular in émigré circles. Maistre said: When there is a vacuum, somebody must enter it. The King failed dismally. King Louis XVI and his miserable liberal advisers, and still more miserable Girondin reformers, were simply human dust, weak, optimistic, reformist, with no understanding of human nature, obviously the ruiners and subverters of society. Then, at a moment of vacuum, the Jacobins did at least do something. At least they killed somebody. They set up guillotines; they performed executions; they let blood flow. That Maistre approved of, because it was an exercise of power, because it held society together, because it made things cohere. He believed in sovereignty. Of course the Jacobins were the scourge of God, sent to punish a godless generation for betraying the faith of their fathers. But still, it is better to do what the Jacobins did and hold France together and make it a powerful kingdom and resist the enemy and crush the opposition of the feeble Prussians or the feeble Austrians – better that than a lot of intellectual jabbering. That is the Fascist note in Maistre.

Similarly, Napoleon was the Corsican monster; he was a fearful usurper, and one must not recognise him. Yet he was a powerful monarch, and power always comes from God, and certainly his title to his throne is no worse than that of Elizabeth of England or William of Orange or the House of Hanover. Maistre was fascinated by Napoleon, just as Napoleon was rather fascinated by Maistre, and each wished to meet the other, except that the King of Sardinia was horrified by any such idea. He was a pensionary of both England and Russia and a victim of Napoleon, and the thought of one of his diplomats meeting the destroyer of mankind plunged the court of Sardinia into absolute terror. Maistre replied with distinct sadness, saying that of course he would not meet Napoleon if the King did not wish him to, but nevertheless he thought this a wrong and short-sighted policy. He said: I see that you regard my proposal as very surprising. Well, I shall serve you to the end of my days, for I believe that the throne is more important than its occupant. As for not surprising you – I cannot promise that.

Maistre stresses tradition, the past, the unconscious, dark forces, not the amiable imaginary attributes of the folk soul, as did its enthusiastic champions – the German romantics – or the champions of the simple life (which he too always praised). On the contrary, he stresses the stability, the permanence and the impregnability of the authority that belongs to the dark mass of half-conscious memories and traditions and loyalties, and the power of institutions in exacting obedience, especially in regard to the supernatural. He lays great emphasis on the fact that absolute rule succeeds only when it is terrifying, and he fears and detests science, precisely because it pours too much light, and so dissolves the mystery, the darkness, which alone resists sceptical enquiry.

In a sense, then, Maistre is a kind of precursor and early preacher of Fascism, and that is what makes him so interesting. Behind the classical mask, behind the classical façade, behind the air of the Grand Seigneur, behind the orthodox Thomism, behind the official complete subservience to the monarchy of his day, which was nothing very splendid or impressive, there is in Maistre something much wilder, much more romantic, much more terrifying. He reminds one of someone like d'Annunzio or Nietzsche – not to seek for later examples. In that way he resembled Rousseau. Just as Rousseau imposed a Calvinist logical strait-jacket upon what was really a burning private lunacy, so Maistre imposes an official legitimist Catholic frame-work upon what is really a deeply violent, deeply revolutionary, ultimately Fascist inner passion.

What made Maistre so fascinating to those of his own generation was that he forced them to look at the seamy side of things. He forced them out of bland optimism; out of mechanical psychology; out of all the smooth ideals of the eighteenth century, which had suffered such a crushing disaster in the

French Revolution. At the end of positivist, optimistic periods of human construction, in which men rise up and say they are about to cure all the world's ills by some economic or social solution, which then does not work, there is always a penchant for reaction on the part of ordinary people, satiated by so much false optimism, so much pragmatism, so much positive idealism, which become discredited by the sheer pricking of the bubble, by the fact that all the slogans turn out to be meaningless and weak when the wolf really comes to the door. Always, after this, people want to look at the seamy side of things, and in our day the more terrifying sides of psychoanalysis, the more brutal and violent aspects of Marxism, are due to this human craving for the seamy side – something more astringent, more real, more genuine, meeting people's needs in some more effective fashion than the rosy, over-mechanical, over-schematised faiths of the past. This is what Maistre provides for his own generation, too. Men cannot live by the ideals he opposed, and Maistre's contribution is a violent antidote to the over-blown, over-optimistic and altogether too superficial social doctrines of the eighteenth century. Maistre earns our gratitude as a prophet of the most violent, the most destructive forces which have threatened and still threaten the liberty and the ideals of normal human beings.

Men may be divided into those who are in favour of life and those who are against it. Among those who are against it there are sensitive and wise and penetrating people who are too offended and discouraged by the shapelessness of spontaneity, by the lack of order among human beings who wish to live their own lives, not in obedience to any common pattern. Among such was Maistre. On the whole he has no positive doctrine, and if he has to choose between liberty and death he rejects liberty. He has his disciples in the twentieth century – Charles Maurras, for example, and Ezra Pound – and although we may disagree with such persons, let us remember that liberty needs its critics as well as its supporters. After all, as in Goethe's *Faust*, Mephistopheles, who criticised the ways of God, is not left altogether without an answer.

NOTES

As in the case of *The Roots of Romanticism*, and for the same reasons (see pp. 148–9 in that volume), I have collected references for quotations together here at the end of the text, identifying the passages to which they refer by page number and opening words.

The reader should be warned that Berlin's quotations from languages other than English are sometimes very free, and can merge into paraphrase. I have not on the whole tried to make them more accurate, since this would often make them less resonant, but I have occasionally given a more literal version in the note. In a few cases, where I happen to know it, I have given a reference for a close paraphrase even though I have withheld quotation marks in the text.

Once again I have recorded my failure to trace a few ostensible quotations. I shall as always be most grateful to any readers who can fill in the gaps, and in future impressions of this book I shall incorporate any information I receive.

The references often depend on the generosity of experts, to whom I am greatly indebted. I fear I may not have kept a record of every single scholar who has assisted me, and I offer my apologies to anyone I have overlooked. Gunnar Beck has helped enormously with Fichte (see the section on that lecture below), Michael Inwood with Hegel, Ralph Locke and Bruce Tolley with Saint-Simon, and Robert Wokler with Rousseau. The Maistre lecture draws again on the invaluable contribution made by Richard Lebrun to 'Joseph de Maistre and the Origins of Fascism', recorded in my preface to *The Crooked Timber of Humanity*. For assistance with individual problems I thank John

Burrow, Andrew Fairbairn, Steffen Groβ, Samuel Guttenplan, Ian Harris, Roger Hausheer (whose general support remains indispensable), Leofranc Holford-Strevens, Andrew Hunwick, Reinhardt Lauth, Richard Lebrun, Ray Monk, T. J. Reed, Philip Schofield, Jonas Steffen and Ralph Walker.

References to multi-volume editions are by volume and page in this form: iv 476.

There are a few editorial remarks interspersed among the references.

Page   *Reference*

Introduction

3   **Bertrand Russell once said**
History of Western Philosophy (London, 1946), p. 226.
Berlin greatly enlivens Russell's presentation of this point.

Helvétius

12   **'As one meditates'**
Discours prononcé dans l'Académie Française, le jeudi 21 février 1782, à la réception de M. le Marquis de Condorcet: i 392 in *Oeuvres de Condorcet*, ed. A. Condorcet O'Connor and M. F. Arago (Paris, 1847–9).

'As mathematics and physics'
Condorcet, *Esquisse d'un tableau historique des progrès de l'esprit humain*: p. 227 in the edition by O. H. Prior and Yvon Belaval (Paris, 1970).

'Morality is the science'
Holbach, *Système de la nature* i. 11.

13   **'I endow thee with sensibility.'**
Helvétius, *De l'esprit* 3. 9

17   **'Do not fight prejudice; use it.'**
This formulation untraced, but cf. Vilfredo Pareto, *The Mind and Society* (London, 1935), vol. 1, *Non-Logical Conduct*, §§ 72–3.

'the language of interest'
De l'esprit 2. 15 (beginning of penultimate paragraph).

'I do not care if men be vicious'
De l'homme 9. 6.

20   **'Woe to us if the masses start reasoning'**
Perhaps a paraphrase of 'when the masses get involved in reasoning, everything is lost', *The Complete Works of Voltaire*, ed. Theodore Besterman and others, cxiv (Banbury, 1973) 155.

20   'The people are cattle'
Untraced, but cf. *Oeuvres complètes de Voltaire* [ed. Louis
Moland] (Paris, 1877–85) xix 208, 623, xxiv 413. Possibly
from a secondary source?

22   'Let us flee from those greedy and cruel animals'
De l'esprit 2. 2.

23   'nature binds by an unbreakable chain'
Condorcet, op. cit. (note to p. 12 above), p. 228.

24   'education is simply'
Holbach, loc. cit. (note to p. 12 above).

'Euclid is a veritable despot'
[Pierre-Paul François Joachim Henri Le Mercier de la
Rivière,] *L'Ordre naturel et essentiel des sociétés politiques*
(London, 1767) i 311.

25   '*bawling* upon paper'
Jeremy Bentham, *Rights, Representation, and Reform:
'Nonsense upon Stilts' and Other Writings on the French
Revolution*, ed Philip Schofield, Catherine Pease-Watkin
and Cyprian Blamires (Oxford, 2002), p. 187.

'nonsense upon stilts'
ibid., p. 330.

Rousseau

27   'Starting from unlimited freedom'
Dostoevsky, *The Devils*, part 2, chapter 7, section 2.

'had produced more effect with his pen'
Herbert Paul recalling Acton in *Letters of Lord Acton to
Mary, Daughter of the Right Hon. W. E. Gladstone*, ed.
with an introductory memoir by Herbert Paul (London,
1904), p. xii.

'Rousseau said nothing new'
Madame de Staël, *De la littérature considérée dans ses*

rapports avec les institutions sociales, ed. Paul van Tieghem (Geneva, 1959), ii 280–1.

32   **'slavery ... is against nature'**
Jean-Jacques Rousseau, *Oeuvres complètes*, ed. Bernard Gagnebin, Marcel Raymond and others (Paris, 1959–95) [hereafter OC], iii 243.

33   **'To renounce liberty'**
OC iii 356.

    'death is not an event in life'
Ludwig Wittgenstein, *Tractatus Logico-Philosophicus* (London, 1922), proposition 6.4311.

35   **'the law of nature'**
OC iii 973.

    'graven on the hearts of men'
OC iii 1001; similarly he says that the laws of custom, morality and public opinion are 'graven, not on tablets of marble or brass, but on the hearts of citizens' (ibid. 394).

36   **'to find a form of association'**
OC iii 360.

    'in giving himself to all'
OC iii 361.

    In a letter to Malesherbes
OC i 1134–8; cf. ibid. 350–1.

39   **'As long as several men in the assembly'**
OC iii 437, 440.

    'penetrates into a man's innermost being'
OC iii 251.

43   **'Man is born free'**
OC iii 351.

44   **'the surrender of each individual'**
OC iii 360.

47   **the right of society to force men to be free**
OC iii 364.

Fichte

At some point after he had broadcast his lecture on Fichte
Berlin annotated the transcript with a view to incorporating numerous additional quotations from Fichte's works.
He probably used this annotated version, and the sheets of
quotations to which his annotations refer (though only
some of these sheets, it appears, survive), in lecturing on
Fichte on other occasions. When I came to edit the
transcript, I discussed the annotations and quotations with
Gunnar Beck, an expert on Fichte, who with Berlin's
encouragement checked them, and suggested further relevant quotations. He also recommended a reordering of the
transcript at one point so that it would follow Fichte's
intellectual development more perspicuously. Berlin accepted this recommendation, which is therefore adopted here;
but he did not revise the text to include more quotations.

I have not attempted to incorporate the additional
quotations myself, if only because this would unbalance
this lecture by comparison with the others, and indeed on
its own terms; it would also go beyond the limits of my
self-imposed general remit. But I give the quotations
below, cued by the last few words of the passage on which
they bear. An asterisk in the text at the relevant point
indicates that supplementary quotations are given hereunder.

References to Fichte's works are to the following editions: *Johann Gottlieb Fichte's sämmtliche Werke*, ed. I. H.
Fichte (Berlin, 1845–6), and *Johann Gottlieb Fichte's nach-
gelassene Werke*, ed. I. H. Fichte (Bonn, 1834–5). These
editions are referred to hereafter as SW and NW.

51 **'It is the individual's right'**
Benjamin Constant, *De la liberté des anciens comparée à
celle des modernes*: pp. 593–4 in Benjamin Constant, *Écrits
politiques*, ed. Marcel Gauchet ([Paris], 1997).

'My system, from beginning to end'
Letter to Karl Leonhard Reinhold, 8 January 1800: J. G.
Fichte, *Briefwechsel*, ed. Hans Schulz (Leipzig, 1925), ii
206.

'To men as they are in their ordinary education'
NW i 4.

53, 61   **'The nature of things'**
OC iv 320: more literally 'it is in the nature of man patiently to endure the necessity of things, but not the ill will of others'.

56   **'desires what he is able to perform'**
OC iv 309.

63   **'I am wholly my own creation'**
SW ii 256.

'I do not accept what my nature offers me'
ibid. Cf. 'Every animal *is* what it is. Man alone is originally nothing. What he ought to be, he must become; and since he must be a being for himself, he must become so through himself' (SW iii 80).

they must serve me
'I want to be master of nature, and she must be my servant; I want to have causal power over her, but she must have none over me' (SW ii 192–3). 'The self is to be absolutely independent, whereas everything is to be dependent upon the self. Hence what is required is the identity [Übereinstimmung] of the object with the self' (SW i 260). This self-determination by the self for itself is defined by Fichte as 'absolute independence from all nature' (SW iv 131). 'Autonomy, our ultimate goal, consists ... in that state of affairs in which everything is dependent upon me and I am not dependent upon anything, where everything that I will occurs in my sensible world simply because I will it to be so, just as in the case of my body, the starting-point of my absolute causality. The world must become for me what my body is for me. To be sure, this goal is unattainable, but nevertheless I should always advance towards it – that is, I should work upon [bearbeiten] everything in the sensible world so that it comes to be a means for the attainment of this final purpose' (SW iv 229). 'Only through voluntary submission of our prejudices and our opinions to the law of truth [i.e. the law of morality] do we first learn to bow and be silent before the idea of a law as such; this law first restrains [bändigt] our selfishness, which the law of morality has to govern. Free and unselfish love for theoretical truth – because it is truth – is the most fruitful preparation

for the ethical purification of our convictions' (SW vi 14).
The moral law is revealed to each man by his conscience
(*Gewissen*). Each man possesses this basic moral faculty,
and it 'commands him to will this and not that, and this
freely and of his own accord, independent from all external
force' (SW vi 11).

66   **lovable but silly**
Cf. Berlin's *The Roots of Romanticism* (London and
Princeton, 1999), pp. 9–10, 139–41. Indeed, in general these
later lectures usefully expand the views on romanticism
expressed here thirteen years earlier.

nature is simply a collection of dead matter
SW i 412–13.

naturam sequi
'To follow nature', the Stoic principle: see, e.g., Cicero,
Laws 1. 56, Seneca, *Letters* 66. 3. 9.

not impinged upon by anything else
'This pure form of our self' alone 'is wholly opposed to the
nature of experience' (SW vi 59). Man's will is governed by
the inner self if it is 'something original [ein Erstes] which
is grounded absolutely in itself and in nothing outside the
self' (SW iv 24: 'Das Wollen, als solches, ist ein Erstes,
absolut in sich selbst, und in nichts ausser ihm Gegründe-
tes'). 'Our sole happiness [Glückseligkeit] on this earth . . .
is free unencumbered self-activity [Selbstthätigkeit], activity [Wirken] springing from our own causal power [eigener
Kraft] and according to our own ends' (SW vi 29). '[Man]
is and must remain free; no authority may prescribe
anything to him other than this law [the moral law –
Sittengesetz] within him; it is his sole law, and it contradicts this law if he allows himself to be governed by
another – the humanity within him will be annihilated and
he will be relegated to the status of an animal' (SW vi 12).
'No one may determine his choice, his direction and his
limits other than man himself' (SW vi 23). 'I cannot allow
any law to be thrust upon me without thereby forfeiting
my humanity, personhood and freedom' (SW vi 13).

67   **has a date and a place**
'Human life and any historical epoch are themselves only

necessary epochs of the One time and the One eternal life
... the life of the *Gattung* [translation problematic:
roughly group, community, species, race]' (SW vii 7).
'[The plan of history] is *this*: that the *Gattung* freely
transform itself through history into the pure expression of
reason' (SW vii 17). 'Individuals now disappear completely
from the view of the philosopher, and all fall together into
the one great community [Gemeine]' (SW vii 14). The
thinking self is 'not that of the particular thinking individual, which could never be independent, but the one and
eternal thinking in which all individuals are mere thought'
(SW vii 55). '*Religion* consists therein ... that all life is
viewed and accepted as the necessary development of the
one, authentic, perfect, moral and blessed life [of the
Gattung]' (SW vii 240–1).

67   **The group – *Gattung* – alone exists**
SW vii 37–8: 'Looking at the matter in truth and as such'
we find 'that the individual does not exist, he should not
count for anything, but must vanish completely; the *Gattung* alone exists.'

'Man only becomes man'
SW iii 39.

'Man is destined to live in society'
SW vi 306. Cf. 'The concept of individuality is [never the
concept of an isolated being but] a *reciprocal concept*
[which] is never merely *mine* but ... always *mine and his,
his and mine*; a common consciousness in which two
consciousnesses are united into one' (SW iii 47–8).

68   **the moral orders [...] of its inner self**
Freedom, man's liberation from necessitation by natural
causality, is no longer the rational self-determination of the
individual, but that process 'whereby the *Gattung* gradually liberates itself through a succession of individuals' (SW
vii 20). 'Man's rational capacity [Vernunftinstinct]', man's
drive to liberate himself from domination by the blind
forces of nature, 'is manifest only in the life of the *Gattung*
as such. It is never manifest in the existence of the mere
individual, whose natural drive aims at self-preservation
and personal well-being' (SW vii 22). 'This one and
unchanging life of reason [Leben der Vernunft] ... is

divided, from an earthly perspective, into a multiplicity of individuals, and therefore appears in its totality only in the one life of the whole *Gattung*' (SW vii 25). 'It is the greatest error and the true basis of all other errors ... when an individual imagines that he can exist and live, think and act for himself, or when someone believes that he himself, the particular person, is the thinking in his thought, since he is merely a single thought in the one general and necessary thought' (SW vii 23–4). 'Reason is manifest solely in the one life of the *Gattung*; if reason does not guide our life, only individuality and selfishness remain. Thus rational life consists in this: that the individual forgets himself in the *Gattung*, ties his life to the life of the whole and sacrifices his life to the whole; and irrational life consists in this: that the individual thinks of nothing but himself and in relation to himself, and seeks nothing but his own well-being ... so that there is but one virtue – to forget oneself as an individual – and only one vice – to think of oneself ... Whosoever seeks enjoyment for himself and thinks of himself and of a living and being apart from within and for the *Gattung* is merely ... a base, little, evil and wretched man' (SW vii 34–5). 'To devote one's life to the *Gattung* means to devote one's life to the idea [by which Fichte refers, interchangeably, to reason or freedom] ... Consequently, the only rational and thus right, good and truthful life consists in man forgetting himself in the pursuit of the idea and seeking no other enjoyment than that of the sacrifice of all other pleasures for the sake of the idea' (SW vii 37).

68 **race, nation, mankind**
'Nothing individual can exist in and for itself; everything can exist only within and for the whole' (SW vii 63). 'The truth of the whole [of the *Gattung*] is confirmed by the fact that its parts are explicable and meaningful solely by reference to the whole ... solely through this whole do the parts exist at all' (SW vii 118). 'The continuation [of life as such and not as the continuation of evanescent existence] ... is promised solely by the independent continuation of his nation: to save her, he must be prepared to die, so that she can live, and he can live in and through her, which is the only life he has ever desired' (SW vii 383).

68 **'Either you believe in an original principle'**
SW vii 374–5. Berlin, as so often, slightly improves on the
quotation, though in essence wording and meaning are
accurate. Cf. 'To have character and to be German is
indubitably the same' (SW vii 446).

70 **'What we need is a leader'**
SW vii 565 (somewhat amplified). Cf. 'Each man who has
the knowledge and the power does not only have the right,
but the sacred duty, to subject men to the yoke of law by
force; a single man [coercing] the whole of mankind, if it so
happens' (SW iv 436). 'Who has the right to be Oberherr?
... The man with the greatest rational insight of his time
and people' (SW iv 444). 'Some day one will come and
must come who, as the most righteous man of his people, is
also their leader; he will find the means to establish a
succession of the best' (NW ii 635).

by a so-called 'organic' process
'The multitude of individuals must be construed as one
indivisible organic whole' (SW vii 157). The true essence of
art, Fichte says, lies in 'its organic unity, as indeed anything
that is of genius, limitless and inexhaustible' (SW vii 95).
The creative, moulding process whereby man's will and
wishes as an individual are brought into unison with his
ethical vocation is placed by Fichte in the hands of the
State. 'The absolute State ... is an artefact, designed to
direct all individual forces to the life of the *Gattung* and
fuse them into one within it' (SW vii 144). 'The end of the
State is ... none other than that of the human *Gattung*
itself, namely that all men's relations be ordered according
to the law of reason' (SW vii 161). In the perfect State
'the individuality of all is dissolved in the totality of the
Gattung' (SW vii 146). 'The end [of the State] is that of the
Gattung' (SW vii 145). 'The end of the State ... is no other
than that of mankind [der menschlichen Gattung] itself,
namely, that all human affairs be governed by the law of
reason' (SW vii 161). 'The State, as the highest governor
[Verweser] of all human affairs, and as the ... guardian of
the ignorant and recalcitrant [Unmündiger], has the perfect
right to coerce the latter for the sake of their own salvation'
(SW vii 436).

the shape of a great nation, or of history
The State now becomes something more than the mere sum

of its parts: 'the conception not merely of an imagined totality ... but of a genuine totality ... not merely of all single individuals, but of their indivisible union [nicht bloß Aller, sondern einer Allheit]' (SW iii 202). In and through the State 'all flow together into One, united no longer in an abstract conception, as a compositum, but truly united, as a *totum* ... Reason is only one, and its representation in the sensuous world is also only one; mankind is one organised and organising totality of reason. Reason was divided into several independent parts, but already the natural institution of the State ends this independence provisionally and melts the separate parts into one whole, until finally morality recreates the whole species into one.

'The posited conception [of the State] can best be illustrated by the conception of an organised product of nature, for instance, that of a tree ... [Each part], as much as it wills its own preservation, must will the preservation of the whole tree, because on that condition only is its own preservation possible ... The whole, therefore, is to be protected first and foremost' (SW iii 203). Each single individual is part of the greater organic whole of the State: 'In the organic body each part continually preserves the whole, and, in preserving the whole, preserves itself; in this way, too, the citizen relates to the State: ... every part, and every citizen, in preserving himself in the position assigned to him by the whole, preserves the whole in its position; the whole returns into itself, and preserves itself' (SW iii 209).

71   **'The idea tries to become action'**
Heine, *Zur Geschichte der Religion und Philosophie in Deutschland*, book 3: vii 294–6 in *Heinrich Heines sämtliche Werke*, ed. Oskar Walzel (Leipzig, 1911–20).

72   **'The world is the poem'**
Josiah Royce, *The Spirit of Modern Philosophy: An Essay in the Form of Lectures* (Boston and New York, 1892), p. 162.

'Kantians will appear'
Heine, op. cit. (note to p. 71 above), vii 351.

'Don't try to suppress or to extinguish the flame'
ibid., 352.

72   **'Thought precedes action'**
ibid.

73   **'For you liberated Germany'**
ibid., 353–4.

        'amidst the nude deities'
ibid., 354.

        Hegel

90   **a slave dragged by the Fates**
Seneca, *Letters* 107. 11, adapting Cleanthes.

        'slaughter-bench'
Georg Wilhelm Friedrich Hegel, *Sämtliche Werke*, ed.
Hermann Glockner (Stuttgart, 1927–51) [hereafter HSW],
xi 49.

        'history is not the theatre of happiness'
HSW xi 56.

91   **'the cunning of reason'**
HSW *passim*, e.g. xi 63.

        'sets the passions to work for itself'
HSW xi 63.

92   **'civil society'**
See especially HSW vii 262–328.

        'the world-historical'
See especially HSW xi 59–65.

93   **'God's march through the universe'**
HSW vii 336.

        a myriad invisible threads
Probably derives from Taine's 'myriades de fils' in *Discours
de M. Taine prononcé à l'Académie française* (Paris, 1880),
p. 24, quoted in Berlin's *Concepts and Categories* (London
and New York, 1978), p. 123, though Berlin usually
ascribes the image to Burke.

94   **the living and the dead and those yet unborn**
Edmund Burke, *Reflections on the Revolution in France*
(1790): 'those who are living, those who are dead, and those
who are to be born' – p. 147 in *The Writings and Speeches
of Edmund Burke*, General Editor Paul Langford (Oxford,
1981–), vol. 8, *The French Revolution*, ed. L. G. Mitchell
(1989).

'concrete'
See especially HSW xvii 52–6.

95   **iron ring**
Untraced.

96   **'Gangrene is not cured with lavender water'**
The German Constitution [not in HSW], § 9: p. 313 in
Georg Friedrich Wilhelm Hegel [*sic*], *Schriften zur Politik
und Rechtsphilosophie* [*Sämtliche Werke*, ed. Georg Las-
son, vol. 7], 2nd ed. (Leipzig, 1923).

'not from the peaceful time-hallowed tradition'
HSW xi 60.

Having quaffed the bitter draught of world history
Paraphrase of HSW xi 119.

97   **'the Emperor – that world soul'**
Hegel to Immanuel Niethammer, 13 October 1806: i 120 in
Briefe von und an Hegel, ed. Johannes Hoffmeister (Ham-
burg, 1952–60).

Saint-Simon

109   **'I write because I have new ideas'**
*Introduction aux travaux scientifiques du dix-neuvième
siècle* (1808): *Oeuvres de Claude-Henri de Saint-Simon*
(Paris, 1966) vi 16; cf. 'Epître dédicatoire à son neveu
Victor de Saint-Simon', *Oeuvres de Saint-Simon et d'En-
fantin* (Paris, 1865–78) [hereafter *Oeuvres*] i 98.

'Rise, M. le Comte'
For this anecdote see Louis Reybaud, *Études sur les
Réformateurs ou socialistes modernes* (1840), chapter 2,
'Saint-Simon et les Saint-Simoniens': vol. 1, p. 67, in the 7th

ed. (Paris, 1864). It also appears in M. G. Hubbard, *Saint-Simon: sa vie et ses travaux* (Paris, 1857), p. 9.

110   **He had been a pupil**
Or so Saint-Simon claimed. According to Frank E. Manuel, *The New World of Henri Saint-Simon* (Cambridge, Mass., 1956), p. 13, 'there is not a scrap of evidence' for this boast.

122   **Therefore (he says very firmly)**
This sentence and the next, which are exceptionally problematic in the BBC transcript, presented difficulties of reconstruction sufficiently severe to justify reproducing them here in their original form:

> and so he says very firmly what we need is simply a State which has become a kind of industrial enterprise, of which we are all members, a kind of enormous limited liability company, unlimited liability perhaps precisely what Burke who in a sense was also historically minded, St. Simon demanded not merely a partnership in all virtue, a partnership in all science, a partnership in all art, although he believes that of course dispassionately, but also a partnership in the most literal sense, in the sense in which Burke statement so to speak decide it was not a partnership – a partnership yes and trade in calico, exactly what Burke denied, a partnership in trade, in commerce, a partnership in industry, a partnership in industry and in the sales of all the human needs of knowledge, without which men cannot get anything done at all.

I am unconfident about my conjectural version of this passage, but I hope at least that the argument is not seriously impaired. If any reader can supply a better solution I shall incorporate it gratefully in any reprint.

'a partnership in all science'
Burke, loc. cit. (note to p. 94 above).

'the best application'
Oeuvres iv 193–4.

125   **'From everyone according to his capacity'**
This is the first part of the epigraph that appeared on the title page of *Le Globe* when the Saint-Simonians owned it.

It continues 'to every capacity according to its work' (which became 'to each according to his needs' in the Marxist version). See Georg G. Iggers, *The Cult of Authority* (The Hague, 1958), p. 151, note 3.

125 **'engineers of human souls'**
In a speech on the role of Soviet writers made at Maxim Gorky's house on 26 October 1932, recorded in an unpublished manuscript in the Gorky archive – K. L. Zelinsky, 'Vstrecha pisatelei s I. V. Stalinym' ('A meeting of writers with I. V. Stalin') – and published for the first time, in English, in A. Kemp-Welch, *Stalin and the Literary Intelligentsia, 1928–39* (Basingstoke and London, 1991), pp. 128–31: for this phrase see p. 131 (and, for the Russian original, 'inzhenery chelovecheskikh dush', I. V. Stalin, *Sochineniya* (Moscow, 1946–67) xiii 410). Gorky used the phrase (without 'human') in a 1934 speech to the Writers' Congress: 'the proletarian State must bring up thousands of excellent "mechanics of culture", "engineers of the soul"'. The idea behind the phrase dates back to the early 1920s, when Mayakovsky made analogies with engineering in discussing the role of the writer.

126 **'the divine Smith'**
Untraced.

the administration, not of persons, but of things
See *Oeuvres* xviii 182–91. This way of putting it is due rather to Engels: see Karl Marx, Friedrich Engels, *Werke* (Berlin, 1956–83) xix 195; xxv 246–7 in the translation in Karl Marx, Frederick Engels, *Collected Works* (London, 1975–), where the relevant passage reads: 'In 1816, [Saint-Simon] declares that politics is the science of production, and foretells the complete absorption of politics by economics. The knowledge that economic conditions are the basis of political institutions appears here only in embryo. Yet what is here already very plainly expressed is the idea of the future conversion of political rule over men into an administration of things [eine Verwaltung von Dingen] and a direction of processes of production – that is to say, the "abolition of the State", about which recently there has been so much noise.' (In *Oeuvres* Saint-Simon's remarks are dated to 1817.)

127   **'You are an aspect of me'**
Literally *'you are* an aspect of *my* LIFE, and *I am* an aspect of *yours'*. See P. Enfantin and H. Saint-Simon, *Science de l'homme: physiologie religieuse* (Paris, 1858), p. 199.

129   **'There is one thing I wish to say to you'**
All except the first sentence of this 'quotation', like the next, is taken from Reybaud, op. cit. (note to p. 109 above, 'Rise, M. le Comte'), p. 84. See also 'Notices historiques I: Saint-Simon', *Oeuvres* i 121–2. (The first part of the injunction in the first sentence seems to be the familiar Christian principle, which Saint-Simon endorsed, but which appears not to have been attributed to him on his death-bed.)

Maistre

131   **'a fierce absolutist'**
Émile Faguet, *Politiques et moralistes du dix-neuvième siècle*, 1st series (Paris, 1899), p. 1

'his Christianity is terror'
ibid., p. 59.

'a slightly touched-up paganism'
ibid. ('un paganisme un peu "nettoyé" ').

'Praetorian of the Vatican'
ibid., p. 60.

'Christianity of terror'
S. Rocheblave, 'Étude sur Joseph de Maistre', *Revue d'histoire et de philosophie religieuses* 2 (1922), p. 312.

'inexorable God aided by the hangman'
E. Quinet, *Le Christianisme et la Révolution française* (Paris, 1845), pp. 357–8.

'slaughter-house'
'[el] matadero del difunto conde José de Maistre'. Miguel de Unamuno, *La agonía del cristianismo*: vii 308 in *Obras completas*, ed. Manuel García Blanco (Madrid, 1966–71).

136   'the heavenly city of the eighteenth-century philoso-
       phers'
       The title of a book (New Haven, 1932) by Carl L. Becker.

137   'In the vast domain of living nature'
       References for quotations from Maistre are to *Oeuvres
       complètes de J. de Maistre* (Lyon, 1884–7 and later
       unchanged impressions). The reference for this quotation is
       v 22–5.

139   'Five or six kinds of intoxication'
       v 34.

142   The Assyrians invented the nominative
       iv 88.

       'What does he mean?'
       ii 338.

143   sheep, who were born carnivorous
       'Dire: les moutons sont nés carnivores, et partout ils
       mangent de l'herbe, serait aussi juste.' op. cit. (note to
       p. 131 above, 'a fierce absolutist'), p. 41.

143   Who is this lady?
       iv 132–3.

144   'In the course of my life'
       i 74.

       'the two anchors of society'
       viii 284.

       Nobody can want as violently
       viii 288.

       'Pugachevs of the University'
       viii 291. Emelyan Ivanovich Pugachev was the leader of a
       peasant and Cossack rebellion crushed in the reign of
       Catherine the Great.

147, 150   'la secte'
e.g. i 407, viii 91, 222, 223, 268, 283, 292 ('une secte détestable qui ne dort jamais'), 311–12, 336, 345, 512–13.

148   **'Who is this inexplicable being?'**
iv 32–3. The reference for the Biblical quotation at the end of this passage is 1 Samuel 2: 8.

'It is as if all his works'
Letter of 8 October 1834 to the Comtesse de Senfft: letter 2338 in Félicité de Lamennais, *Correspondance générale*, ed. Louis le Guillou (Paris, 1971–81), at vi 307.

150   **the perpetual hideous grin**
iv 208–9: 'Ce *rictus* épouvantable, courant d'une oreille à l'autre, et ces lèvres pincées par la cruelle malice'.

151   **'The principle of the sovereignty of the people'**
ix 494.

INDEX

Compiled by Douglas Matthews